TRAVELLING WITH CHILDREN

A Parent's Guide

Need — 2 — Know

Catherine Cooper

Travelling with Children – A Parent's Guide is also available in accessible formats for people with any degree of sight loss. The large print edition and ebook (with accessibility features enabled) are available from Need2Know. Please let us know if there are any special features you require and we will do our best to accommodate your needs.

First published in Great Britain in 2011 by
Need2Know
Remus House
Coltsfoot Drive
Peterborough
PE2 9JX
Telephone 01733 898103
Fax 01733 313524
www.need2knowbooks.co.uk

Need2Know is an imprint of Bonacia Ltd.
www.forwardpoetry.co.uk

Contents

Introduction 5

Chapter **1** **The Right Holiday** 9

Chapter **2** **Plane, Train or Automobile?** 17

Chapter **3** **Babies and Toddlers** 27

Chapter **4** **Package Beach Holidays and**

Theme Parks 37

Chapter **5** **Camping and Caravanning** 47

Chapter **6** **City Breaks** 55

Chapter **7** **Off the Beaten Track** 65

Chapter **8** **Skiing** 75

Chapter **9** **Luxury, Cruises and Spas** 85

Chapter **10** **Holidays on a Budget** 95

Chapter **11** **When Things Go Wrong** 107

Help List 113

Introduction

Having a baby changes your life – no one will argue with that. But being a parent and taking holidays with your children doesn't mean you can't have the holiday you want – whatever that might be. You can still go backpacking, visit luxury hotels, go on adventurous or sporty holidays or visit that city you always wanted to visit. If you plan carefully, you and your children will be able to enjoy almost any kind of holiday together.

Changing your expectations

Admittedly, once you are a parent there are some ways in which your holidays are going to change forever. While you have small children you are probably not often going to get a lie-in. But with a little planning, you can still get what you want from your holidays. If you want to read a book on the beach for two hours without being interrupted, choose a destination with a kids' club. Perhaps you want to be pampered at a luxury hotel? There are many that are fully geared up for young children. Maybe you want to go backpacking? Fine – just make sure you don't try to cram in too much. Or that city you always wanted to go to but never got around to visiting? Go anyway – just intersperse the museum visits with some more child-friendly activities and check if the hotel will lend you a high chair. The world is still your oyster.

What children want

Research has shown that when children are asked what they enjoyed most about their holidays, almost all will say they enjoyed being with their families. Children aren't impressed by exotic destinations. They don't generally mind if it rains every day or if the accommodation isn't up to scratch. So while you should, of course, plan your holiday with the needs of your children in mind, what you want to get out of the holiday is just as important. Chances are, if you enjoy your holiday, your children will too.

'Being a parent and taking holidays with your children doesn't mean you can't have the holiday you want – whatever that might be.'

Family-friendly?

There is now a raft of family-friendly tour companies and destinations offering everything for kids, from the basics of a cot and highchair to round the clock nannies and miniature bathrobes. But a destination doesn't have to labelled 'family-friendly' to be thoroughly enjoyable for families.

For example, Marrakech in Morocco isn't a destination which would necessarily spring to mind as a suitable holiday destination for a young family. But the Moroccans' love of children and its famous main square full of performing monkeys, snakes and acrobats and a riot of unfamiliar sounds and smells, along with the opportunity to ride on a camel can make it a holiday to remember for even quite small children. The trick with family travel is sometimes to think about where you would like to go, and only then think about how best to do it so your children can enjoy the trip too.

How do I choose?

There is a huge range of holidays to choose from and a wealth of information out there that can make choosing a holiday seem quite daunting. There are so many questions – where to go and when? How to travel? Who to go with? What to do when you get there? What to pack? This book aims to guide you through the decision-making process, as well as helping you ensure you get the most out of your holiday from beginning to end.

No one can tell you what type of holiday to take – that is a very personal decision. But this book can help you think about what holiday will suit you best and how to get what you want from your holiday. It will suggest travel companies which are especially suitable for young families and discuss what type of holiday suits what type of family. It will also deal with what to do when things go wrong, as well as providing resources for finding out more about successful travel with children. Throughout the book real parents will be talking about their own experiences of the type of holidays you might be considering to help you make your choice.

Bon voyage!

Disclaimer

Information contained in this book was correct at the time of going to press, however facilities and offers are subject to change – please check before booking.

This book offers many suggestions for family-friendly holiday companies and destinations based on the author's personal experiences and those of others, but this is by no means exhaustive.

Chapter One
The Right Holiday

The world is your oyster when it comes to choosing a holiday and the choice can be quite overwhelming. How do you decide where you want to go and what you want to do? Here are some points to consider.

What do we want from our holiday?

It sounds obvious, but it is important to think about what you actually want from your holiday. Do you want to spend a week lying on a beach, or would you rather also spend some time sightseeing or taking part in a sporting activity? Do you want to spend all your time as a family or would you also like some time alone or as a couple, apart from the children? Think about what elements are most important to you and make sure the holiday you plan can include these.

Where to go?

Very young children generally don't care where they go on holiday – what they remember is spending quality time with their parents. If your children are a little older, you will need to think about a destination where they can have some fun – but remember they may not be impressed by exotic locations.

If you have teenagers going with you, you might want to choose a holiday in which you can allow them a little independence. Take the ages of your children into account when choosing your holiday – just because one type of holiday suited you five years ago doesn't mean it will necessarily still be as much fun now.

'I used to be a right globetrotter but found that when Ava came along I preferred to have holidays that were predictable. We've got a static van in west Wales and that's where we've had most of our recent holidays.'

Cath.

UK, short haul or long haul?

This decision will probably depend on a combination of your budget, the ages of your children and what is most important to you in a holiday.

UK holidays

If it is your first holiday with a small baby, you might decide to stay in the UK where it is easy to take baby equipment with you and everything is more familiar. However, UK holidays can work equally well for families with older children.

The advantages are you can travel to your destination by car which is generally cheap and easy – plus it means you can take everything with you. There are no language or currency issues and chances are it won't be too hot! A UK holiday can work particularly well for young children who don't like too many changes to their routine.

There are countless interesting places to visit in the UK, whether you want a beach, sightseeing holiday or simply a theme park to entertain the children. The UK also offers enough variety that you can choose somewhere which feels very different from where you live.

'Remember that if you are travelling abroad, everyone will need an up-to-date passport, including babies.'

Short-haul holidays

Once you decide you are going to go abroad, a huge range of options open up. The advantages of taking a holiday abroad, depending on where you go, can include more predictable weather and the chance to experience a different culture. Some people feel more like they have 'had a break' if they have been abroad.

In summer, sun-seekers have a huge choice of where to go on a short-haul holiday. But even in winter the sun is never that far away – the Canary Islands are warm all year round and Egypt can also be a good option for some winter sun.

Remember that if you are travelling abroad, everyone will need an up-to-date passport, including babies. Details of who to contact to apply are included in the help list.

Long-haul holidays

Long-haul holidays are likely to be more expensive than other types of holidays because of the longer flight and larger airfare. However, before discounting this type of holiday as too expensive it is worth noting that for some destinations – for example India or Thailand – the actual cost of living once you get there will be much cheaper.

The main advantages of long-haul holidays are often hotter climates and greater cultural and geographical differences. However, these differences will be lost on very young children, so if you are planning the trip for your children rather than for yourselves, it might be worth waiting until they are an age at which they can better appreciate it.

While flying with a small baby might seem daunting, you do not need to buy a plane ticket for children under two, so budget-wise it might be worth taking that long-haul holiday while your baby is still a baby.

If you are planning a long-haul holiday it is important to check the weather and any vaccination requirements. Both these points will be covered in greater detail later in the book.

'If you are planning a long-haul holiday it is important to check the weather and any vaccination requirements.'

Booking

Whatever kind of holiday you are booking, check what children's facilities are on offer as they may vary widely. Websites such as www.babyfriendlyboltholes.co.uk and companies such as www.totstotravel.co.uk offer accommodation which is specifically child-friendly. It can be convenient to book through child-friendly operators such as these, but it is not essential. If you are booking through a non-specialist operator simply make sure you are entirely clear on what children's equipment they can and cannot provide and ask if the property is safe for children.

Accommodation

Think about what sort of accommodation will suit you best. If you want a break from cooking and cleaning, you might prefer a hotel. If you want to prepare meals when you want to, especially if you have young children, you might prefer to go self-catering. Self-catering accommodation can also work well if you don't want to share a bedroom with your children or you have young children who need to go to bed early.

> 'Self-catering means you can put the children safely in bed at night and then sit out with a glass of wine and an adults-only barbecue!'
>
> Sarah.

Case study

Sarah prefers self-catering holidays:

'We opt for the self-catering option as it means you can put the children safely in bed at night and then sit out with a glass of wine and a BBQ adults only! Also, it allows us to eat out if we want to, make picnics, give them lunch and then put those in need of sleep down.

'Last year we rented a house through a company called Tots to Travel, who were fab for our needs – they provided two cots, two highchairs, cot linen, the pool was very securely fenced off, the house had a playground, steriliser, blender, plastic spoons, bowls, paddling pool, etc – everything we needed for two very small children and a toddler. For us, self-catering works perfectly – not to mention restaurants can often be a waste of money if the kids don't eat what's put in front of them and can't sit at the table for longer than 10 minutes.'

What to spend?

It is important to decide how much you want to spend and stick to it. There is no point going on a holiday you can't afford as you will simply spend your time worrying about it. It is important to think not only about the upfront cost of booking the holiday but also about how much money you will need to spend while you are there.

Facilities such as the Post Office Holiday Costs Barometer and Mercer's Cost of Living Survey (see help list) will give you an idea of how much items such as food, drink and activities might cost at your holiday destination. You can also check the current exchange rate at www.xe.com, but it is important to remember that this may change.

If rigidly sticking to a budget is important to you, you might like to consider an all-inclusive holiday. While what you pay for the holiday may be higher, it is much easier to keep control of what you spend while you are away.

When to go?

While summer is the traditional time to go on holiday, prices are high and resorts are busy so it can be worth considering travelling at a different time of year. Even in winter it is possible to have a sunny holiday without travelling too far.

If your children are not yet at school it is wise to try to travel outside of school holidays, when prices are much lower and holiday resorts much less crowded.

Taking children out of school

How you feel about taking your children out of school might depend on what stage they are at. A child in the early years of primary school may arguably have less to lose by taking a week off than an older child about to take an important exam.

While taking children out of school to go on holiday is discouraged across the board, different schools will have different policies, and some will even fine parents if a child does not attend school. In theory, you can be prosecuted if your child does not attend school but this is usually reserved for extreme cases.

If you are considering taking a holiday during term time it is usually best to check what the school's policy is and approach the head teacher for permission.

'Even in winter it is possible to have a sunny holiday without travelling too far.'

'We used to holiday with the grandparents when the kids were smaller, but now find it more fun to go away with friends and everybody has a ball.'

Kate.

Who will you go with?

For some families, holidays are all about spending quality time alone as a family. Other families prefer to go on holiday with friends or members of their extended family. There can be great advantages to this – for example if you are travelling with the children's grandparents, they will probably enjoy spending time in a fun location with their grandchildren while also giving you the freedom to spend some time alone or as a couple.

If you travel with a family which has children of similar ages, the children will have ready-made playmates and chores such as cooking and shopping can be shared. You can even take it in turns to babysit.

However, it is important to choose your holiday companions carefully. Ideally they should not only enjoy the same kind of holiday as you, but also have a similar approach to bringing up children. It will be very difficult if one set of children are allowed to eat ice cream all day and stay up late while the others are expected to finish their vegetables and be in bed on time.

Summing Up

There is a huge range of options when it comes to booking a family holiday. The most important thing is to think about what you want from your holiday and only then think about where best to go and what type of holiday to take. Points to consider are:

- What is your budget?
- Do you want to stay in the UK or go abroad?
- Do you want to travel short haul or long haul?
- Do you want a beach holiday, active holiday, sightseeing or a combination?
- Who will you travel with?
- Who is going? Will there be something to keep everyone happy?

Chapter Two

Plane, Train or Automobile?

A key feature of any holiday is obviously that it will involve some travel. The form of travel you prefer may perhaps influence your choice of holiday destination if you feel strongly about carbon emissions or particularly favour one form of transport over another. In some cases, for example if you are travelling long haul, or if you have booked a package tour, there may be no choice of how you travel. If you are travelling within the UK or Europe there are usually choices to be made. But first, there are some general rules which apply however you choose to travel.

Timing

When travelling with children, and especially babies, the journey will be a lot easier for everyone if you try to keep as close to the children's usual routines as possible. Try to avoid very early mornings and late nights and plan when and where you will feed the children en route.

While travelling at unsociable times of day can be cheaper, especially on planes, think carefully before you book about whether saving a few pounds is going to be worth dealing with over-tired and grumpy children for a couple of days.

Extra time

Always allow much more time than you think you will actually need to get to an airport, train station or ferry terminal. Getting from A to B always takes longer with children who may walk slowly, drop things, perhaps need a nappy changed or throw a tantrum. Little is more stressful than having to rush through an airport terminal because you are pressed for time dragging both luggage and a screaming toddler.

Children aside, trains can be delayed or you can get caught up in bad traffic. Missing your plane or train will not only be a very bad start to your holiday, but buying new tickets can also be very expensive or sometimes impossible. It is much better to arrive early and have plenty of time to perhaps have a snack and take everyone to the toilet or even just enjoy some shopping.

'When you're flying long haul it's important to check on exactly what comprises a baby carrier on the aeroplane and how you'll be expected to secure baby during landing and take-off.'
Lynley.

Air travel

Since the arrival of low-cost carriers, air travel is often the most cost-effective and fastest way to get to a short-haul or medium-haul destination. However, it is not always the most enjoyable. Air travel can be quite hard work with an active toddler as they will be expected to stay in their seats.

Conversely, it can be easier than you might imagine to fly with a very small baby. On long-haul flights, you can request a bassinet so you will not have to sit with the baby on your lap all the way, and it can make it easier for you both to sleep. It's important to book one of these early though as they are generally allocated on a first-come, first-served basis. It is also worth checking what type of bassinet it will be, as there are several different types.

Lynley says: 'On some planes I have had a fold-down table, on which the staff secure something that looks like a bouncy chair. You strap baby into this. Now this is great for short periods, but you can't put a baby in that position for more than two hours at a stretch, which is very annoying on a 12-hour flight. Other times it was more like a box, which I much preferred.'

Luggage restrictions

Airlines, especially budget airlines, have very strict luggage restrictions. The good news is that every child aged two or more is entitled to their own baggage allowance, even if you have to carry their bag. Sometimes under-twos will also be allocated an allowance – check this with your airline.

Many budget airlines (and some non-budget ones) will only allow one item of carry-on luggage per person. Some add a weight restriction to this, and some will also insist that any purchases made at the airport must also fit into your hand luggage.

If you have too many items of hand luggage, or they are too heavy, you will be made to put them in the hold and may be charged a fee. Check the luggage allowance on your airline's website carefully before you pack. It can be handy to buy a set of inexpensive luggage scales to make sure you don't go over the limit.

Some airlines will charge per piece of hold baggage and all will set a weight limit per bag – some will also set a baggage weight limit per person. Again, check your airline's policy before you travel.

Buggies and baby paraphernalia

Most airlines will allow you to take a buggy in addition to your usual luggage allowance. Some will also allow a car seat, but most low-budget carriers will charge for this as if it were an extra bag.

Some will allow your child to sit in a car seat on the plane if they are aged over six months. The seat will have to conform to certain criteria (including size) and it is important to check what these are with the individual airline before you go. If your child is under two, it will also mean booking an extra seat. Under-twos will still have to sit on your lap for take-off and landing, even if you have booked an extra seat.

Some airlines, including (at the time of writing) Thomsonfly, First Choice and British Airways also allocate a hand luggage and cabin bag allowance for under-twos, while a low-cost airline may not allow you to take both a nappy bag and a handbag. Again, it is important to check with your specific airline before you travel.

'Make sure you adhere strictly to the luggage allowances.'

What is forbidden in hand luggage?

The threat of terrorist attacks has meant there are now stringent rules about what you can carry in your hand luggage. You cannot take anything sharp, including scissors, nail files, tweezers or knitting needles, and your child cannot take their favourite toy gun!

Liquids (including creams, sun cream and make-up) must be in bottles or containers of less than 100ml and must be placed in a clear plastic bag around 20cm by 20cm. You cannot take larger, half-empty containers. Anything larger than 100ml will be confiscated at security.

Duty-free goods and any other liquids you buy once you are past security will be allowed on to the plane as hand luggage. There are no restrictions on carrying liquids in hold luggage.

Baby food, milk and medicines

Baby food and milk are exempt from the 100ml rule but you may be asked to taste them when you go through security. Essential medicines in larger bottles are also exempt but it is wise to bring a note from your GP or decant into a smaller bottle for the flight if you can.

How many seats should I buy?

You will need to buy a full-priced seat for any child aged two or above. Under-twos who have not been bought a full-price ticket do not get their own seats but still need to be booked on to the plane and bought a ticket, albeit for a much-reduced price (usually around £10 to £20).

Most airlines will allow you to buy a seat for a child over six months if you choose to and feel you want the extra space. This option may not always be available online – you may have to call the call centre. One sole adult will not usually be allowed to travel with more than one child under two.

Priority boarding?

Many budget airlines do not allocate seats but allow passengers to purchase the right to be one of the first on to the plane. Check whether your airline lets families travelling with young children board first (most do, but some don't) before splashing out on this.

It is also worth noting that at airports where you go from the departure gate to the plane in a bus, while you will be one of the first on to the bus, you won't necessarily be able to get on the plane first.

In practice, the cabin staff will not allow a small child to sit on their own and will move other passengers if need be, so unless you feel you want to board first purely for convenience, it isn't absolutely necessary.

Boarding passes

Be aware that some airlines will charge you extra if you have not printed off your boarding pass before you get to the airport. Check the booking conditions carefully.

Flying while pregnant

Flying while pregnant does not usually present any problems, but it is wise to check with your GP or midwife before booking your flight, especially if you have experienced any complications during your current or any previous pregnancies.

If you are 24 weeks pregnant or more, the airline may require you to have a note from your GP confirming you are fit to fly. Some airlines will not allow women who are more than 32 weeks pregnant to travel (some set the limit at 36) in case they go into labour. Check with your airline before booking.

Tips for travelling by plane

- Make sure you adhere strictly to the luggage allowances – trying to reorganise bags and stuff excess weight in your pockets at the airport is stressful.

- You will not always get your buggy back at the plane door – sometimes it will be on the luggage carousel. Request when you get on the plane that you have it back at the door but be prepared for the fact that it may not be possible. It can be worth taking a baby sling or carrier as well as the buggy.

- Try to bottle or breastfeed babies on take-off and landing as it can help reduce pain in their ears. Older children can be given a sweet to suck – or try to get them to yawn.

- If you are travelling low-cost take food – food onboard is usually expensive and not child-friendly. Take plenty of healthy, non-sticky snacks too.

- Consider using a 'meet and greet' service at the airport where they take your car away and bring it back for you. This costs a little more but avoids having to negotiate crowded airport shuttle buses with buggies, children and luggage.

- Visit http://flyingwithchildren1.blogspot.com for in-depth info about flying with children written by a mother and ex-flight attendant.

Train

Within the UK or even within Europe, taking the train can be a good option. All packing restrictions are avoided, travel times can be more flexible and while you are actually travelling, you will have more space and you and your children will be able to move around to a degree. It can be less tiring and also much faster than going by car.

Disadvantages include, depending on where you are going, you may have to hire a car or get a taxi once you reach your destination unless you take the Motorail (a European service where your car comes on the train with you). It can be more expensive and take longer than flying or driving.

Tips for travelling by train

- It is possible to get cheaper fares by booking in advance.

- At weekends you can upgrade to first class for a small fee on some lines – this will get you a larger seat and often free drinks and snacks.

- Make sure you are not booked into a 'quiet carriage' with young children.

- Some trains carry 'Kids' packs with colouring books etc – ask the ticket inspector or at the buffet car.

- Even if you don't travel by train often, it can be worth buying a Family Railcard – you can often save more than the price of the card on just one journey.

Car

Travelling by car has many advantages – you can set off when you like and can take as much stuff as you can fit in with you. The disadvantages are that someone has to drive, which can be tiring and stressful and you are at the mercy of traffic problems – especially at peak holiday times. Long journeys can be very boring as in-car entertainment is limited and some children get car sick.

If you are hiring a car, make sure you pre-book child seats (but watch out, as this can be expensive) or take your own. If your children are big enough to use booster seats www.bubblebum.co.uk have an inflatable seat and www.trunki.com have a seat which doubles as a child's backpack.

Tips for travelling by car

- Make sure everyone has been to the toilet before you set out.

- Plan several stops.

- Consider taking a picnic if you are travelling on the motorway – service stations can be expensive and the food uninspiring. In summer, if you take a picnic there is often an outdoor playground at service stations where the children can play while you eat.

'Flying for us is financially restrictive – not the cost of the flights so much, but the cost of hiring a big enough car to fit three car seats in. So we tend to drive to France.'

Sarah.

- If your children like to sleep in the car and you are confident you can stay awake, you might consider travelling at night.

- Audio books and seat-back DVD players can make a long journey much less painful for everyone.

- Reading in the car is not recommended – it can exacerbate car sickness.

Games to play

- I Spy.

- Who can spot a…red car, motorbike, yellow lorry, dog, etc.

- Counting as high as you can using numbers spotted on number plates.

Ferry

'Always allow more time than you think you will actually need.'

Taking a ferry can be a good choice if you want to go to mainland Europe but want to take your own car with you. If you are going to the South of France or Spain you might consider taking a longer ferry journey (e.g. to St Malo or Santander rather than Calais) as this will shorten your drive.

There is much more to do on a ferry than in a car and you and your children can move around rather than being confined. As well as restaurants, bars and shops, many have play areas for kids. The main disadvantage is being at the mercy of the weather – you may get a rough crossing or ferries may be cancelled.

Tips for travelling by ferry

- Look out for offers and promotions which are often run by ferry companies via national newspapers.

- Prepare for seasickness – take travel sickness pills and some people use acupressure bands for the wrists. You or your children may not be affected, but it is best to be prepared.

- Ferries can be very large. If you have older children, arrange a meeting place in case anyone gets lost.

Coach

Travelling by coach is often cheap compared to other forms of transport – sometimes as little as £1 between towns within the UK, and long-distance coaches usually have toilets, air-conditioning and even TVs. It is also possible to take coach trips into Europe – although long coach journeys with small children can be very tiring!

Disadvantages include not being able to move around or have as much space as you would on a train and not having the flexibility you have in a car. For older children who are able to entertain themselves, perhaps with a hand-held computer game, coach travel can be a good, affordable option.

Visit www.nationalexpress.com for information about coach travel within the UK and www.eurolines.com for information about European coach travel.

Summing Up

Don't forget that the journey is part of your holiday. The most important thing is to allow plenty of time to keep it as stress-free as possible. With a little planning, it can actually be enjoyable – honest!

Things to take on every journey:

- Plenty of non-sticky snacks (e.g. carrot sticks, BabyBel, small packs of raisins) and drinks in bottles instead of cartons.

- Wet wipes, even if your children are beyond the age where they usually need them and plastic bags to dispose of them (and other rubbish).

- Rewards (e.g. sweets or cheap toys) which can be given at intervals for good behaviour.

- Small, non-precious toys with no parts which can easily be lost. Colouring or puzzle books are good for planes, trains and ferries. Small notebooks and pens are also excellent as makeshift toys for simple games and drawing.

- Mobile phone in case of emergencies or simply a delay.

- If you have a baby, more nappies, milk and food than you think you could possibly need.

Chapter Three
Babies and Toddlers

There are many special considerations to planning a holiday with a baby or toddler – especially if you are taking them for the first time.

Expectations

Taking your first holiday with your baby is very exciting and should be a joyous time for everybody. But it is important to realise that this holiday will be unlike the ones you took as a single person or couple. This doesn't mean it can't be fun, and doesn't even mean it can't be relaxing – just that it won't be the same.

'Going with friends or family can add to the fun.'

Case study

Mary tells us how she found her first holiday with her baby:

'It's not that I loved it or hated it – it was just hard work. Not what I was used to as I had to do all the looking after baby jobs that I did at home but without the convenience of being in my own house where everything was to hand. So I was pretty much still on duty all day like at home. It then dawned on me that my idea of what a holiday was would have to be re-framed.'

Who will do what?

Talk to your partner or travelling companions about your hopes for the holiday. Discuss if you will take turns to look after the children while each has some time alone or if you plan to do everything together. If you are self-catering, think about how the cooking and chores will get done. If you are travelling with friends or extended family, it can be a good idea to draw up a babysitting or cooking rota. This may sound boring but may save arguments or resentment later on.

When can I take my baby on holiday?

In theory you can take your baby on holiday as soon as you like after the birth, and babies only have to be seven days old to fly. But you might find yourself better able to enjoy a holiday once you have got used to being a parent and perhaps your baby has started to settle into some kind of routine.

Pregnancy

It is risky to book a holiday for after the birth while you are still pregnant. The baby may have unforeseen complications and you may need to attend medical appointments. Similarly, you do not know how you will feel after the birth; you may find you prefer to stay closer to home for a while. You may, of course, feel like going on holiday, in which case you can book one once the baby is born.

What do I need to take?

The first time you travel with a baby, you will be amazed at how much more luggage you will have. It is important to find out exactly what can be provided at your destination – there is no point in taking more than you have to. You could also consider using www.bebebel.co.uk who will deliver a package of your chosen branded baby goods direct to your accommodation.

Checklist of things to take, or check if they are provided

- Cot.
- Bedding for cot – many places provide the cot but not the bedding.
- Highchair.
- Changing mat.

- Steriliser (if bottle-feeding).

- Baby monitor.

- Hand blender (if you need to make purees).

- Washing machine (so you know how many sets of baby clothes to take).

- Nappies, wipes, bags for dirty nappies and changing bag.

- More changes of baby clothes than you think you will need (unless you want to do laundry).

- Buggy and/or baby carrier (check which is most appropriate for your destination – you may want both).

- Feeding equipment as appropriate (breastfeeding cushion, bottles and teats, formula).

- Simple first aid kit, including plasters and infant paracetamol in sachets (see chapter 7 for a list of what to include).

- Muslin squares.

Feeding

Babies need to be fed frequently and will become very unhappy if they have to wait. It is important to consider this both when planning your journey and your holiday.

Breastfeeding

The great thing about breastfeeding while you are travelling is that you don't need to take anything with you to do it. However, if you are going abroad, especially to further-flung places, it is important to check how breastfeeding in public is viewed in the country you are visiting. Visiting the 'parents abroad' section of parenting websites can be a good way of finding out information like this.

- Wherever you are going, you might prefer to take a shawl or pashmina to allow you to feed more discreetly.

'Check how breastfeeding is viewed in the country you are visiting.'

- If you are in a city where you feel uncomfortable feeding in public, the ladies' toilets of a smart hotel can be a good place to go (although you might feel you have to buy an over-priced drink at the bar afterwards).

- La Leche League advises that you do not need to supplement breastfeeding with water even when you are in a hot climate. However, you should keep an eye on your baby's nappy. If it is drier than usual or his or her urine is a darker colour than usual, you need to feed more often. It is also important that you make sure you drink enough as well.

Bottle-feeding and baby food

- For short trips, disposable bottles can make feeding a lot easier as there is no need to sterilise. It can also be easier to buy formula in pre-measured sachets to avoid taking huge tins and having to measure out messy powder on the go.

- Ready-made up formula is also available and can be convenient, but is bulkier than the sachets and may cause you problems going through airport security. However, it is very useful during journeys where it may be impossible to prepare fresh formula, or if you have concerns about the water at your destination.

- Cabin staff will heat bottles and baby food on planes but make sure you test the temperature before giving it to your child – it often comes back far too hot.

- If you are staying in anything other than self-catering accommodation, check that there will be somewhere where you can heat up milk or baby food.

- If your baby will only drink a certain brand of formula, it is worth checking if it is available at your destination and taking a supply with you if not. You will usually be able to find this out by calling the formula company's customer service line.

'When they're little, the best holidays are simply ones where you have a little bit of living space, and are self-catering so you can always get some food for them, and have something simple and easy within a short walking distance like a beach on which they can potter around for ages.'

Lynley.

Where will we stay?

Self-catering

When you are travelling with a baby or toddler many families find a 'home from home' environment works best for them and so many choose self-catering accommodation. The advantages of self-catering are generally that you have more space, your child can have their own room and you have all the facilities you need for preparing food as and when you want to. Having your own space also means you don't have to worry about how your child is behaving. Some good starting points for baby-friendly self-catering accommodation can be found in the help list.

Going with friends or extended family can add to the fun, as well as meaning that you get to share cooking and cleaning, and can also babysit for each other.

Hotels

If you choose your hotel carefully, your holiday can be more restful than a self-catering one, as there is no cooking and cleaning to be done! However your child will usually be sharing your room, which will usually mean that unless you choose a hotel with a baby-listening service which you are happy to use, you will have to go to bed at the same time as your child. The other potential problems with hotels include worrying that your child is disturbing other guests, lack of indoor play space and lack of facilities for taking meals and preparing food at unorthodox times of day.

However, all these potential problems can be circumnavigated by choosing a hotel that specialises in families. See the help list for some suggestions.

It is also perfectly possible to enjoy a stay with children in a mainstream hotel – but it is important to ask a lot of questions about their facilities and think about the logistics of your stay before you go.

'If you are self-catering, think about how the cleaning and chores will get done.'

Bed and breakfasts

Bed and breakfasts (B&Bs) can be a good option for families or can be a terrible option. Some will be very geared up for children while others will not be child-friendly at all.

Advantages can include that they are usually small and, as long as they have a guest lounge, you may feel comfortable leaving your children asleep upstairs while you go downstairs with a baby monitor to watch TV, chat or have a quiet drink. Some may have a guest kitchen where you can heat food and milk. As with hotels, do your research and choose carefully.

Camping and motorhomes

Camping has many of the advantages of self-catering, although arguably in less comfortable surroundings. If you choose your site carefully there may be facilities such as shops, pools and kids' clubs.

Motorhomes can be an ideal solution if you want to visit several places easily. These options will be discussed in more detail in a later chapter.

Safety

Small, immobile babies are fairly easy to keep safe on holiday. Safety becomes much more of an issue once you have a baby who crawls, a toddler or a young child.

Ask questions

One of the most important contributions you can make to your child's safety on holiday is to ask questions before you go so you can be confident that the accommodation is safe and go prepared for any potential hazards.

'When I arrive I check for any obvious dangers, get the kids accustomed to the place and try to get them to understand where the dangers are and to be careful.'

Danielle.

Swimming pools

If there is a pool, check if there is a safety fence. In some countries, such as France and Australia, pools must be either fenced or alarmed. An alarm will only operate once someone (or something) has fallen in, so a fence with a self-closing gate is much safer. For communal pools, ask if there is a lifeguard.

If you are staying in a villa with a private pool, one adult should be designated 'pool supervisor' at any time when children are near the pool. This avoids children being left unattended near the pool with everyone assuming someone else is watching them.

Plug sockets

You might want to consider taking some plug socket covers with you on holiday if you have a toddler with curious fingers. UK plug socket covers can be bought from any high-street retailer selling baby equipment. If you are travelling abroad you can buy the right type for international plug sockets very cheaply from online retailers such as Amazon.

Locks

Remove keys from any doors where a child might be able to lock themselves in.

Balconies

If your room has a balcony, look closely at the height of the railings and the gaps between them. Legislation on balcony safety varies greatly from country to country and it is often very difficult to check if a balcony will be safe before you arrive.

If you have any concerns at all about whether the balcony is safe for your children, ask for a ground floor room. If this is not possible you may have to resign yourself to keeping the door firmly closed, but this is far from ideal. If you can, try to book accommodation where you are confident any balconies will be safe.

While you are on holiday take very great care that no children are ever left alone on the balcony. Make sure no chairs, tables or anything else which can be used to climb are left near the edge of the balcony.

Sun

One of the greatest dangers to babies and small children on holiday is sunburn. Make sure you take plenty of high-factor sunscreen and reapply it regularly. Children and babies should also wear sunhats and sunglasses with high UV protection – there should be a sticker which tells you how much protection the glasses offer when you buy them.

UV sun suits are great for babies and small children as they protect large parts of their bodies from the sun without the need to apply sunscreen.

Try to keep your children out of the sun between 11am and 3pm when it is at its strongest. If you are on the beach, make sure you have some shade available. Make sure both you and your children drink plenty of water or fruit juice.

For more information about sun safety see, *Skin Cancer and Sun Safety – The Essential Guide* (Need2Know).

Getting lost

Talk to your children about what they should do if they get lost. Point out lifeguards, policemen, hotel staff or other people they could approach for help. Tell them if they can't see any of these people to ask a lady with children for help.

If you are out and about, put your name and mobile phone number on a piece of paper inside your child's pocket and if he or she is old enough, explain to them why you are doing it.

For younger children and while on the beach, identification wrist bands such as those sold by www.identifyme.co.uk are ideal.

Car seats

If you are hiring a car, make sure you have reserved a car seat, specifying the child's age, in advance. Car seats from hire companies can vary in quality and you may feel more comfortable taking your own. If you are flying, remember that this will generally be considered as part of your luggage allowance.

What else do I need to think about?

Remember that babies and toddlers like familiarity. Take a few small, non-precious toys that they will recognise. If you are taking their favourite sleepy toy, look after it during the journey and give it to them at the other end – that way it is much less likely to get lost. Try to get a spare if you can.

Try to stick as closely as possible to their mealtimes and bedtimes as at home while allowing the odd late night and treats here and there. Don't try to cram too much in – make sure you all have some downtime.

Summing Up

Going on holiday with babies and toddlers can seem daunting. It certainly takes more preparation (and more luggage) than travelling without children. The key thing is to ask as many questions as possible before you go and plan carefully to make sure you have everything you need. Once that is done, all that is left to do is enjoy yourself!

Chapter Four

Package Beach Holidays and Theme Parks

These type of holidays are some of the most common taken by families. A package holiday, whether you go to the beach or a theme park, generally means that everything – your flights, transfers, accommodation and sometimes your food – is all organised by one company. There can be both advantages and disadvantages to this.

Advantages of a package holiday

- Your transport will be arranged from the airport or ferry terminal all the way to your accommodation, so you won't need to take public transport or taxis and any problems caused by delays should be sorted out by the tour operator.

- It can be easier to budget as there are fewer elements to pay for – but it is important to check exactly what is included when you book.

- Package holidays work well for people who like to be sociable on holiday – there will probably be other children, often kids' clubs and other children's activities as well as company for you if you want it too.

- Many companies will organise excursions away from the resort which can be easier and (sometimes) cheaper than trying to organise it yourself.

- If you have a problem while away there will be a holiday rep who should help you to sort it out.

'As a mum I want a good rest on holiday while my children want to enjoy themselves – activities and entertainment that has been planned for you can be brilliant.'
Linda.

Disadvantages

- Travel times can be inflexible (but it depends who you travel with).

- You can feel like you are being 'herded'.

- It can be difficult (although usually not impossible) to do your own thing.

- It can be very crowded in peak season.

Linda, who enjoys package holidays with her husband and twin daughters says: 'As a mum I want a good rest on holiday while my children want to enjoy themselves – activities and entertainment that has been planned for you can be brilliant. While some may say this makes you part of a "herd" – I don't care – if that herd is having a great time! As a family we are quite sociable and I like to see my daughters joining in, say at a disco and making friends.'

Mother-of-one Kelly, disagrees. She says: 'I hate that package holidays are just that – one-size-fits-all holidays that someone else is in control of. I prefer to book my own flights, find my own accommodation and tend to go to places that other families don't really go.'

'If you can, travel outside of school holiday periods.'

How should I get a good deal?

If you can, travel outside of school holiday periods. You can often get early booking discounts if you can plan ahead and book early. It is also possible to get 'last minute' discounts by booking just before you travel. This strategy is more risky though as it depends entirely on what holidays remain unsold. If you go down the latter route you may find your choice is quite limited, while if you book early you should be able to choose the holiday you want.

Do your research. Get several brochures from your local travel agent or spend time browsing Internet sites. You may find that different companies are offering holidays at the same hotel for different prices – or offer different facilities.

You may want to consider going all-inclusive. While the initial cost may be higher, it makes it much easier to budget in advance. The downside is you are restricted to eating within the resort – unless you want to pay twice.

As the flight is often a large part of the cost, you can sometimes have a two-week holiday for not very much more than the price of a single-week holiday and occasionally, bizarrely, two weeks can even be cheaper.

Where should I go to the beach?

Spring and autumn

In spring and autumn, Greece, Tunisia and Cyprus can be good choices as the warm weather stays a little longer than in countries closer to home.

Summer

If you are travelling in summer, you don't have to go very far to get to a beach with a nice warm climate. France, Spain and Portugal are all very popular package holiday beach destinations although the list is almost endless.

For something a little more unusual but still not too far away, you could consider Croatia, Montenegro or Bulgaria.

Winter

In winter the Canary Islands and Egypt are good choices for some sunshine on a budget. If you are happy to pay more and go further afield there are many options, such as the Caribbean or Asia.

These are just a few ideas – there are many, many other options. You can use websites such as www.weather.co.uk to check average temperatures and rainfall at different times of the year all over the world.

Don't forget to ask friends for recommendations and spend some time browsing websites and brochures when deciding where to go. Many holiday operators' websites have whole sections devoted to helping you choose where to go on holiday which can be very helpful.

'You can sometimes have a two-week holiday for not very much more than the price of a single-week holiday.'

How should I choose a travel company?

Think about what you want from your holiday. Here are some points you might like to think about according to what is important to you.

- Do they offer activities for children or kids' clubs?
- Do they offer sporting activities?
- Do they offer excursions?
- Is there evening entertainment?
- Is it a reputable name?
- Check that it is ATOL (Air Travel Organisers' Licensing – a financial protection scheme for air holidays) or ABTA (The Travel Association – aiming to maintain high standards of trading practice within travel companies) registered.

'Smaller companies may be able to give you a more personalised service and offer greater flexibility.'

Remember that many of the facilities on offer will vary from destination to destination as well as from company to company, so it is also important to check what will be available at your specific holiday location.

The main large operators in the UK which offer a wide range of holidays of many types, include First Choice (the more family-orientated branch of Thomson), Thomas Cook, Cosmos and Virgin. Other operators to consider, especially if you are interested in sporting activities or want a kids' club, include Club Med and Mark Warner.

There are also many smaller travel companies. In some instances smaller companies may be able to give you a more personalised service and offer greater flexibility. The most important thing is to shop around to find the option which is most appropriate for you.

Single parents

Going on holiday as a single parent can be expensive, as many packages will charge the same for one adult as two.

> **Case study**
>
> Single mother of one Sally, who blogs at www.whosthemummy.co.uk says:
>
> 'I'm sick of getting invited to family-friendly places where the price is (say) £500 plus £50 per child. No discount whatsoever for single parents. So holidays that are dead affordable for two-parent families are stupidly expensive for us.
>
> 'We were invited to review a Keycamp holiday – that company offers a discount for single parents which is unusual.
>
> 'Also I found the kids' clubs amazing – if you're a single parent, holidays can be stressful because you get no downtime – you're the driver, cook, entertainer and organiser. My daughter Flea did four or five sessions at the kids' club and it gave me time to chat to other adults, and also just sit on the beach and read books. Bliss.'

Others find it helps to go on holiday with another single parent. Lynley says: 'My friend is a single parent, and so we've done the holiday thing together. I'm not single but the summer hols are long and my husband can only get so much time off.

'It works out pretty well then as we make up the "two adults and two kids" package. The big problem though is the sleeping arrangement. Two bedrooms are usually a double bed and two single beds.'

There are also several companies which specialise in holidays for single parents, as well as a website where you can meet up with like-minded single parents to holiday with. See the help list for details.

Taking friends

Some parents allow their children to take a friend along. This can work well, particularly if your child is an only child, or if there is a large gap in the ages of your children.

If you plan to do this, make sure you meet the parents of the friend before to discuss boundaries, discipline and most importantly, money. What aspects of the holiday will you want them to pay for and how much should their contribution be?

Check that the friend has their own holiday insurance or can be covered on yours. If you are going abroad, take a letter signed by both parents giving permission for you to take their child with you, otherwise you may risk getting turned back by border control.

Kids' clubs

One attraction of package holidays for many families is that many of them offer kids' clubs. These can serve the dual purpose of keeping the children happy and giving you a bit of time off to sunbathe, sightsee or just enjoy some peace and quiet.

Some parents like the idea of a kids' club but are worried about actually using one. Here are some questions you should ask before deciding if a kids' club is the right thing for you and your children.

- What ages of children do you cater for?
- Do you have different activities for different age groups?
- How many children are there per adult?
- Do the people looking after the children have any qualifications?
- What kind of activities will my child be doing?
- Is there somewhere my child can sleep?
- Can children eat there? What sort of food is provided?
- How does the signing in and out procedure work?
- Can I stay for a while to settle my child in?
- Can I drop off and pick up my child when I like or are there set hours?
- If my child is upset or ill what is the procedure?
- Can you deal with special needs or allergies?

How can I help my child settle into kids' club?

Most holiday kids' clubs are very well organised, but both you and your child will feel happier if you have made some simple checks.

- Ask if you and your child can have a look around the club before you plan to leave your child there and try to meet some of the carers.

- Have a look at what the children in the club are doing during your visit. Do they look happy and interested? Is anyone who is upset being comforted? Does it look like a safe environment? If you have any concerns or questions, ask.

- Some children settle more easily if you stay with them for a while the first time you drop them off, but for many, a brief, cheery goodbye kiss and a clear statement about what time you will be back to pick them up is better.

- Leave your child just for a short period the first time and try to pick a day when they are planning an activity at the club you know your child will enjoy.

- Ensure the staff have your phone number in case of emergencies.

- Make sure you are not late to pick them up. Chances are that after one visit they will be desperate to go back.

'Most holiday kids' clubs are very well organised.'

Theme parks

Theme parks come in all shapes and sizes. Some are ideal for a day out while other, larger ones have hotels onsite and are suitable for weekend stays or even longer.

Linda says: 'I loved theme parks when I was a child and I still love them now. I relish the adrenaline rush of a white-knuckle ride and so do my children. We love getting soaked on water rides and screaming our heads off when being thrown around at massive heights. Yes – theme parks are noisy and busy – but they are also crammed full of attractions that are genuinely enjoyable and the laughs you can enjoy together can make memories that last a lifetime.'

What ages are they for?

Most theme parks will have a wide range of rides suitable for everyone from children aged just three or four (some even younger) right up to white-knuckle rides for daredevil adults. Some offer 'meet and greets' with 'live' cartoon characters for younger children and even babies can enjoy a Disney parade.

Have a good look at individual theme parks' websites which generally list every ride and attraction available before deciding where to go.

What about babies?

While babies will be too small to enjoy many of the attractions to the full, on the whole, babies are well-catered for at theme parks as regards changing nappies and areas for heating food. Buggy hire is also often available – this can also be useful for tired older children before the end of the day.

At Disney theme parks their 'Baby Switch' scheme allows parents of small children to take it in turns to go on the scarier rides while the other one stays with the baby or child without having to queue twice.

'Most theme parks will have a wide range of rides suitable for everyone.'

Express passes

Some theme parks offer passes which let you jump the queues and get on the rides more quickly. Queues for the main rides can be very long (up to four hours at some parks at peak times) and can be well worth the money if you are planning to go on all the roller coasters and the most popular rides.

Bear in mind that at most parks express passes can only be used on the major rides and may not help you jump the (sometimes still lengthy) queues on rides for younger children. Check which rides are covered before you buy.

What accommodation should I book?

For larger theme parks, such as Disney and PortAventura near Barcelona, it is possible to book travel, accommodation and park entrance tickets as one package.

Parks regularly have special offers and promotions, particularly for very young children or outside of school holidays, so this can be an economical way of booking.

It can be convenient to have your accommodation onsite and to be able to take advantage of services such as the Disney Express, where if you are arriving by Eurostar you are able to leave your bag at the station to be taken to your hotel so you can get straight on the rides.

The other option is to book accommodation away from the park and travel in. This can be very cost-effective, especially if you camp or rent a self-catering apartment. It can also make it easier to see more of the local area rather than just the theme park.

Some theme park ideas . . .

- Gulliver's World – theme parks especially for children aged two to 13 so ideal for little ones. There are three parks around the UK – it is possible to camp at one.

- Wunderland – a theme park in Germany built in a disused nuclear power station complete with rides inside the old cooling tower. As much ice cream and chips as you can eat is included in the entry price.

- PortAventura – near Barcelona, has its own enormous water park and is on the coast. Ideal for a little bit of everything, especially in the hotter months.

- Butlins – there are three sites around the UK, and it has been revamped over recent years to try to shed its 'Hi-de-Hi' image and offers entertainment for the whole family.

- Disneyland – there are sites in America, France and Hong Kong. Great rides and fantastic parades. Frommers have produced various 'unofficial guides' to several of the Disney parks which can help you get the most of out your stay – see the book list for details.

This is just a small selection of parks which also offer accommodation – there are many, many more. Most have very informative websites where you can find information about rides and attractions to select the one most suitable for you.

Summing Up

Package beach holidays and theme parks may not be for everybody. For sociable families who like lots of activities on holiday and want their booking and travelling to be as seamless as possible, they can be ideal. They can also work well for parents who want to spend a little adult time away from their children.

However, it is worth remembering that all package holidays are not the same and even if you prefer a quieter type of holiday, if you choose your travel company and destination carefully a package beach holiday could work well for you.

Chapter Five

Camping and Caravanning

Camping and caravanning are popular choices with families for many reasons. These types of holidays can be very reasonably priced and offer many options – from camping in a basic tent in a field to staying in a luxury mobile home with many facilities nearby.

There are also more unusual options available, such as yurts and tree houses. Whatever kind of camping experience you are looking for, with a little bit of research you are bound to find something that will suit you.

Is camping for me?

With almost any form of camping, there is going to be a certain degree of 'roughing it'. Staying in a tent is not the same as staying in a comfy cottage, bed and breakfast or hotel.

Not only will you have to do your own cooking and washing up, you might have to cook over a tiny stove and then trek to the other side of the campsite to wash up. You won't normally have your own bathroom or shower and will probably have to walk to the toilet (even in the middle of the night) or take a bucket.

Upsides of camping include a feeling of getting back to nature and away from the normal routines of life.

Some families enjoy taking camping holidays with other families. Mother of three Tamsin says: 'We go camping a lot with five or 10 other families. Kids run free. Parents get pickled and laugh a lot. Group holidays are a fab way to relax – everyone is entertained, you can peel off when you want to be just with family, and get other people cooking.'

If you have never camped before, or never camped with your children before, it can be wise to book a short trip for your first go. Camping with children can be tiring – it is difficult to make a tent truly dark, so they tend to go to sleep late and wake up early and it is not always possible to get the same 'down time' as you may be used to at home. Having the whole family living in such close quarters can also, sometimes, be trying.

But almost without exception, children love the novelty of camping. There is no reason not to take a baby camping, but you might want to think about the practicalities of feeding and changing before you decide where to book your camping trip and exactly which type of accommodation to choose.

What kind of campsite should I choose?

As with any other type of holiday, it is important to think about what you and your family want from your holiday before deciding what type of site to choose. There is a wealth of options but here are some basic types to consider:

Large commercial sites

There are a large number of operators both in the UK and abroad running chains of large parks, many of which have excellent facilities. Operators include Keycamp, Eurocamp and Canvas Holidays and there are many more.

These sites can be ideal for families who like to be sociable on holiday and mix with other families. They can be particularly good for families with teenagers or children with a wide range of ages, as there are usually a variety of organised activities and discos for all ages. Many large sites have their own private beaches and swimming pools and most will have facilities such as shops and restaurants.

Most sites offer a range of pre-assembled tents, mobile homes and sometimes also bungalows or chalets. Accommodation will usually come kitted out with cooking and eating facilities as well as camp beds – you may or may not be expected to bring your own bedding. It is important to check exactly what is and isn't included so you know what to take with you.

'With almost any form of camping, there is going to be a degree of "roughing it".'

Disadvantages of this type of site include that they can be crowded and noisy. They are not generally suitable for families who like to feel they have 'got away from it all' on holiday.

Case study

Charlotte, aged 11, describes why she enjoyed her trip to a Siblu mobile home parc in France:

'Our holiday home was big with an awning so we could eat outside on the decking every day.

'There was lots to do – the pool and slides were really good and the changing cubicles were fun because they were made to look like beach huts. We played table tennis and crazy golf as well.

'The children's shows were funny and you could watch them while you were eating outside of the restaurant. The thing I liked the best was when we hired bikes and rode through the forest to the beach. We took a picnic and stayed there all day, playing football on the sand with some of the French children.'

Small, basic campsites

Instead of going to a site where your tent is provided and set up for you, you can load up your car with a tent and camping equipment and do it all yourself.

Many small sites have excellent facilities while others will have very few at all. Again, it is important to think about what suits you best. Some sites will allow barbecue and/or campfires, others won't.

The advantage of this type of camping is you can choose a smaller, quieter site and you may feel the experience is more authentic. The disadvantages are there will probably be fewer facilities and you will need to make your own entertainment.

Mother of two Ally said: 'Our camping criteria consists of small campsites with a defined boundary (so young children can wander unsupervised), no loud evening entertainment, decent sized flat plots, shade. A swimming pool is nice too.'

If you are taking this type of holiday with babies or young children it is important to think about timings – you will probably not want to arrive late and have to put up a tent in the dark, while also trying to deal with hungry, tired or fractious children.

The *Cool Camping* series of books and website www.coolcamping.co.uk are excellent resources for choosing a small, independent campsite both in the UK and abroad.

What to take

'Take a big tent so your kids have somewhere to play even if it rains.'

Alison.

- Tent, groundsheet, tent pegs.
- Sleeping bags.
- Bedding rolls, airbeds or camp beds.
- Extra blankets – even the warmest places can get cold at night!
- Towels.
- Camping stove, gas canisters, camping kettle, saucepans, cutlery and crockery. Chopping board and sharp knife.
- Food, salt and pepper.
- Washing-up bowl, scrubbing brush, washing-up liquid.
- Tea towels, washing line, clothes pegs.
- Coolbox.
- Matches, corkscrew, bottle opener.
- Portable loo.
- Several torches and spare batteries.
- Flip-flops for the shower.
- Toilet rolls and toiletries.
- Wellies, unless you are going somewhere where it definitely won't rain.
- Lots of plastic bags.

Wild or free camping

For those who really want to get back to nature and away from it all, it is possible to take your tent, caravan or motorhome and set up for the night somewhere which isn't a campsite at all.

The rules on wild or free camping are a little woolly. In theory, in England at least, all land belongs to somebody and permission should always be sought where possible. But as long as you are sensible and camp away from houses and fields with animals and only for a few days at a time, chances are you will be fine, although there is always the chance that you will be asked to move on.

Website www.go4awalk.co.uk suggests the Lake District and Snowdonia as ideal places for wild camping where you are unlikely to come across any problems. Wild camping is discouraged in some areas of the Peak District and sometimes banned altogether.

In Scotland you have a legal right to wild camp on hill land as long as you are at least 100m from a road.

There are many resources for finding free camping sites in America such as www.freecampsites.net. To find out about free camping rules in other countries, or if you are in doubt wherever you are, ask at the local tourist office.

Free camping is possible with young children or babies. However, you will need to be extremely organised and make sure you have packed for every eventuality if you plan to pitch up somewhere remote.

'Camping doesn't have to mean squatting in a field over a billy can.'

'Glamping'

Some people like the idea of camping but don't like the idea of totally roughing it. Others want to sleep under canvas but want something a little different from the experience too – so-called 'glamping' (glamorous camping) might be the answer.

Below are a few ideas which offer camping with a difference. It is by no means an exhaustive list – ask around or go online and you will find plenty more.

- Featherdown Farms – several farms around the UK which offer luxury tents with wood burning stoves for heating and cooking, canopy beds and a flushing toilet. Facilities vary from location to location but typically include an 'honesty shop', egg-collecting and other animal-based activities and bike hire. Some offer home-cooked food and smoke-barrels for cooking.

- Yurts – a yurt is a circular, Mongolian tent. There are several places both around the UK and abroad which offer yurts.

- Tipis – similar to yurts, from native America. Also available in several locations across the UK and abroad.

- Tree houses – Canvas Holidays offer tree houses which sleep up to six in the Loire Valley.

- Exotic – Jardins D'Issil just outside Marrakech in Morocco offer a luxurious under-canvas haven from the bustle of the city. The tents are air-conditioned and there is also an infinity pool on-site.

Caravans, motorhomes and static vans

Some families find static vans, caravans or motorhomes a good compromise between camping and a hotel, cottage or apartment. You can feel you are in the great outdoors but you also get to have your own toilet and shower and slightly more comfortable accommodation.

With a caravan or motorhome, the great advantage is you can travel as and when you choose, taking all your things with you. This can be particularly useful for parents of babies and young children who have a lot of paraphernalia and like a familiar setting. As with camping, you can choose where to stop (large or small site, or somewhere else entirely) according to your tastes.

Lynley says: 'When my son was a baby the best holiday we had was travelling around British Columbia in an RV (recreational vehicle). My son was three months old and my stepson was 16. With a baby in tow, an RV meant we had everything to hand all the time – a microwave, fridge etc, plus separate sleeping areas. I could get up at 5am to feed my son and watch dawn come up over the Rockies. At night we could sit outside with a glass of wine while he slept. Brilliant.'

'We love our camper van, so easy to pack up and go where we want, and stop when and where we want to.'

Fiona.

Static vans (sometimes also called mobile homes) can be found on some campsites. There are also sites which specialise in this type of accommodation. These sites will tend to have the same kind of features, advantages and disadvantages of a large campsite. There will usually be facilities such as shops, restaurants, pools and entertainment, but they may feel crowded and noisy at peak times.

It is also possible to find unusual caravans such as gypsy roulottes to stay in both the UK and abroad – Canvas Holidays offer them in France and you can find others via Internet searches.

Examples of operators which offer static van accommodation in the UK include Shorefield Parks and Haven, and in Europe, Siblu. Most will offer different sizes of van and levels of facilities (e.g. TVs and DVD players) according to your wants and budget.

Chalets, lodges and other accommodation

If you want facilities close at hand and a campsite-type atmosphere without actually staying in a tent or caravan, many large campsites (including some of those mentioned above) also offer chalets or lodges.

These can offer a greater amount of space and comfort and can be particularly suitable for those with babies and young children, particularly if they still need to take daytime naps. Some, such as the lodges at some Shorefield Parks, even have private hot tubs.

Center Parcs is another option for families looking for this type of accommodation. Center Parcs are traffic-free and enclosed and can work well for families who want to allow their children a little more independence in a safe environment. Each park also has an Aqua Sana spa to help keep Mum happy.

'Many large sites have their own private beaches and swimming pools.'

Summing Up

Camping doesn't have to mean squatting in a field cooking over a billy can. These days it is possible to find tents with almost all the comforts of a modern home – at many campsites you can even hire TVs, microwaves and fridges.

Camping isn't for everyone. But if it is something you enjoy, there is no reason to think you have to give it up just because you now have children. Having children can even be the excuse you need to try it for the first time!

Chapter Six

City Breaks

A city break may not be the most obvious choice for a holiday with young children. Chosen carefully, many cities, with their parks and museums, have a great deal to offer children. For children who aren't used to cities, even travelling on a bus or underground train can be a treat in itself.

Planning your city break

Which city to choose and what to do when you get there is a very individual choice, but this chapter will give you some points to consider. When planning your trip, browse the tourist office websites for any city you are planning to visit – they will have all the information you need about travel, attractions and accommodation to help you make your choice.

When to go

Check what the weather will be like when you plan to go. Visiting a city in high summer can be exhausting. Similarly, a city break in the freezing cold is not usually much fun. For much of Europe, spring or autumn can be a good bet.

Some European cities, such as Paris, almost shut down for the summer. While this can mean fewer crowds, it may also mean that some of the attractions you may want to visit won't be open. Check before you go.

How long to go for

When visiting a city, especially with children, less is often more. City breaks usually involve more walking and general activity than a typical holiday and can therefore be quite tiring. Four days in a city is usually plenty – for smaller cities, two days may be enough. You could consider combining a few days in a city with a few days in a more relaxing environment not too far away, such as at the beach or in a cottage in the countryside.

Where to stay

Bear in mind that cities are noisy. If your children (or indeed, you) like to go to bed early, you probably won't want to stay right in the heart of things as you may have chosen to before you had children.

'When visiting a city, especially with children, less is often more.'

Have a look at the transport links in the city. It may be both cheaper and quieter to stay in a suburb slightly out of the city on a convenient metro or bus route. It can also be less expensive and mean you have larger accommodation.

You may find it more convenient to rent an apartment rather than a hotel so you can prepare your own meals and have more space. If you are going somewhere hot, check that your accommodation has air-conditioning.

Tips for making the most of your city break

Plan ahead

If you are only visiting for a few days, you want to make the most of your time. Have a look at the tourist office's website and buy a guidebook. Make a list of what you want to see and draw up a rough itinerary.

This may sound boring but it will mean you can avoid travelling back and forwards across the city more than is necessary. Many children also like to know in advance what they will be doing, especially when they are in an unfamiliar environment.

If there are restaurants you particularly want to try or shows or exhibitions you want to see, book ahead, especially if you are visiting during the holiday season.

If you are keen to see a very popular attraction, for example the Eiffel Tower, it is usually best to go first thing in the morning. Don't expect to be first in the queue however early you get there though!

Mix children's and adults' activities

Just because you are travelling with your children does not mean you have to spend your entire trip in theme parks and ice cream parlours.

Most children will usually enjoy museums, galleries, historic houses or churches (and especially castles) as long as you keep the visits fairly short. Modern art museums can work particularly well for children – there is usually a lot of space and they will often find some of the exhibits interesting, even if it is for different reasons than the artist planned. Some museums and galleries have children's programmes on certain days or have children's worksheets to help keep their interest.

Don't expect young children to appreciate art or a historic building in the same way as you might – allow them to enjoy it in their own way, as long as they don't touch anything which they are not allowed to or disturb other visitors. Museums which have outdoor exhibits which allow children to run around or sculptures which can be touched can also work well.

Use the 'carrot' approach – tell your children that once you have been to the art gallery you will go to the water park later, or similar.

'Most children will usually enjoy museums, galleries, historic houses or churches (and especially castles) as long as you keep the visits fairly short.'

Take the tourist trains

Many popular tourist towns operate little road trains which take a tour of the town, usually accompanied by a commentary recorded in several languages about the history of the town.

Taking one of these tours can be an excellent way to start your visit. It allows you to get your bearings and work out the geography of the town, as well as seeing some of the main sites and hearing a little about the history of the town without too much walking. Meanwhile, as far as your children are concerned, they are simply enjoying a train ride. Open-top bus tours and river trips can also work well for the same reasons.

Visit the tourist office

The tourist office should be one of your first stops when you arrive in a town or city. Ask about any special offers – in many towns there are special transport deals for tourists, or some sell passes which can be bought for a small sum which offer discounts at some of the town's major attractions.

Most offices will offer free maps and leaflets about the town's attractions and latest events. Staff will also be able to answer any questions you may have and suggest activities suitable for your children.

'The tourist office should be one of your first stops when you arrive in a town or city.'

Take breaks

Being constantly active is tiring, especially for children. Don't try to cram in too much. Try to plan your days so there is some downtime – perhaps an afternoon at the cinema, or an hour or two playing in a park or feeding ducks.

Wander around – but have a plan

As well as taking the advice of the guidebooks, it is sometimes fun to simply take a wander and see where you end up. However, with young children this can quickly turn into having to cajole fractious children who are whining about being tired or bored.

The easiest way to 'wander' with children is to have an end destination in mind (perhaps an ice cream parlour) for them to focus on while you explore the streets between point A and point B. With older children, in many cities (for example, those in Holland), exploring by bike can work well.

Other considerations

- Buggies – for very young children you will need to take a buggy. For some cities, if you are planning a lot of walking, it can be useful to take a buggy even if your child doesn't habitually use one anymore. For other cities (e.g. Venice), a buggy might be a hindrance and you would be better off with a baby carrier. Think about what you are going to be doing and plan accordingly.

- Breastfeeding – if you are breastfeeding, how is breastfeeding in public viewed where you are going? The tourist office or embassy should be able to tell you. If feeding in public is not acceptable, take bottles or plan where and when you will feed your baby in advance. This is covered in more detail in chapter three.

- Transport – would a car be useful where you are going or is the traffic heavy and parking difficult? Take this into consideration when planning your trip.

- Clothing – make sure everyone has comfortable, worn-in shoes, a raincoat and a sun hat.

Where should I go?

Your choice of city will depend on many things – how far you want to travel, what your interests are, the ages of your children and your budget. Below are a few suggestions of cities which can work well with children with details of some attractions suitable for the whole family.

Barcelona

- Easily accessible by budget airlines and with beaches actually within the town, Barcelona is a great destination for almost any time of year except the height of summer when it is very hot.

- Highlights children will love include two cable cars and of course the beach! Parc Guell is full of Gaudi architecture as well as offering plenty of space for the children to run around and a spectacular view of the city. Gaudi's Sagrada Familia – the famous unfinished church – is strange-looking enough to capture most children's interest but you need to be there very early to beat the queues. There are also several modern art museums (including ones devoted to Miro and Picasso) which everyone can enjoy.

■ Take a walk down La Rambla to watch the living statues at work and order tapas – you can include some child-friendly ones such as omelette but also get them to try some more adventurous ones too – they might even find something they like.

Marrakech

'The main square Djeemaa el Fna is packed with fascinating things for children to watch – acrobats, monkeys, henna artists and snakes.'

■ Marrakech perhaps isn't the best place to go with a baby – it's too crowded to be very buggy-friendly and there isn't much in the way of baby facilities – but for families with children aged about three and up who are looking for something a little different it is ideal.

■ It is easily accessible by budget airlines. The best times to visit are early spring or late autumn although even in winter it generally remains pleasantly warm – in summer it is scorchingly hot.

■ The Moroccans adore children and are quite tactile – if you or your children aren't prepared for them to be cuddled and patted this probably isn't the place for you. It can also be difficult for unaccompanied women, particularly if they are blonde.

■ The main square, Djeemaa el Fna, is packed with fascinating things for children to watch – acrobats, monkeys, henna artists and snakes. You can take a ride in a caleche (horse-drawn cart) or on a camel. If you have time you can go out into the Atlas Mountains and trek while your children ride on a mule. To cool off, visit the Oasiria water park.

■ If you are travelling with young children you will probably find it easier to stay in one of the Western style hotels in the Hivernage or the Palmeraie rather than in a riad in the medina which tend to be very peaceful and not ideal for noisy children.

Amsterdam

- Calm and peaceful, Amsterdam is easy to walk (or cycle) around. You can visit Anne Frank's house, take a boat ride, hire pedalos and go to the zoo.

- There is also a Jewish children's museum where kids can take part in baking and arts and crafts and there are several places where you can go to see windmills.

- A nice thing to do with children who are old enough to cycle is rent bikes and take the bike paths along the Amstel river and have a picnic near the windmill there.

- Young children will love the Kinderkookkafe (www.kinderkookkafe.nl) in Vondelpark where they can cook their own cakes and pizzas (with a little adult help).

- Alternatively, head out to Zaanse Schans where the windmills still work and you can even stand inside them. The science centre NEMO is also well worth a visit. Just outside Amsterdam and accessible by bus there is a large theme park, Duinrell.

Louise, who visited Amsterdam with her two sons, says: 'One evening my son played football with some local kids who all spoke a bit of English. The pace of life is really laid back.'

Paris

- Paris is easily accessible from the UK by train or plane and can easily be combined with a trip to Euro Disney, which can be reached easily via the RER train.

- Children, especially those old enough to climb steps, will love the iconic Eiffel Tower. On a hot day rowing on the lake in the Bois de Boulogne can be fun as well as Le Jardin d'Acclimatation, which dates from 1860 and is accessed by a little train. Not to mention the Tuileries Gardens with its rides and huge Ferris wheel.

- The Musée de la Magie, Cité de Science and Grevin Wax Museum are also well worth a visit.

Copenhagen

- Accessible directly from the UK by ferry, Copenhagen has pretty squares and beaches nearby and most families with young children are utterly enchanted by the Tivoli Gardens.

Case study

Becci Combes, founder of the Girls' Travel Club, on her trip to Copenhagen:

'I reckon Copenhagen has to be one of the best cities for kids, especially at Christmas.

'There are free places on buses for kids and pushchairs, and there are lots of kids' menus in all the restaurants, plus high chairs, but best of all is Tivoli Gardens.

'It has rides, funfairs, lasers, fairy lights, fireworks, ice skating, mechanical pixies in a winter wonderland, braziers to warm your hands while you eat hot apple dumplings with jam and drink Glogg.

'The National Gallery has art activities on for kids at weekends, then there is an Experimentarium where they can push lots of buttons, and a planetarium and an aquarium too, plus great hot dog stands!'

Las Vegas

- Much more than just a gambling Mecca, there are several zoos, parks, a waxworks museum and a huge aquarium in Las Vegas. Children will love the lights and reproductions of everything from the Eiffel Tower to the Egyptian Pyramids.

- Other attractions include Adventure Dome, America's largest indoor theme park, and the Tournament of Kings, a dinner show in which the showroom is transformed into King Arthur's Arena.

- Las Vegas is also a good jumping-off point for Los Angeles, San Francisco, Disneyland and many other places.

Camilla, who visited Las Vegas with her children says: 'We loved the Bellagio water fountain show and one day caught a plane out to the Grand Canyon – I'll never forget how awesome that was!'

These are just a few ideas and recommendations. But almost any city will have something to offer children during a short trip – it's just a question of finding it.

Salzburg

Salzburg can be great fun for slightly older children who aren't going to be scared by caves. You can visit ice caves and salt mines, some of which feature slides, mine trains, sledging and even a raft trip across a subterranean lake.

Back in the open air you can ride the cable car, visit the zoo and Natural History Museum, which also has an aquarium and a science centre with 80 interactive exhibits.

Music lovers can take a tour of the shooting locations from *The Sound of Music* and Mozart's birthplace which includes a 'Day in the Life of a Child Prodigy' exhibition.

Case study

Alan, who visited Salzburg with his three children then aged 11, 9 and 6 says:

'Salzburg is a small, walkable city, with lots of fun things to do in the city itself and in the immediate area – things like ice caves and salt mines that you don't normally encounter.

'We visited the Bad Dürrnberg mine at Hallein, taking a train to Hallein then a cable car to the mine, into which you ride on a little train, and then walk along tunnels which run across the border from Germany to Austria. We also enjoyed the Eisriesenwelt Höhle – ice caves – at Werfen, also via a cable car, with a wonderful log cabin café at the top.'

Summing Up

A city break with children is not usually the most relaxing holiday and needs careful planning. However, it can be exciting and even educational for the whole family. It is possible your children will also gain more insight into a different country and culture by visiting a city than by going to a beach or staying out in the countryside.

Some cities are packed with museums and children's attractions. But even those which aren't obviously child-friendly are almost certain to have some hidden gems. Go, explore, and see what you can find. Things to consider include:

- Decide where you want to go.
- Check what the weather is likely to be like.
- Browse the Internet and read guidebooks.
- Decide which attractions you would like to visit.
- Book your accommodation and travel.
- Plan your itinerary – remember to leave some downtime.
- Have fun!

Chapter Seven

Off the Beaten Track

Having children doesn't have to preclude you from taking holidays off the beaten track. Many families successfully go backpacking, on safari and on extended holidays with children of all ages. But just as with any other type of holiday, when you are travelling with children, you may want to plan slightly differently than if you were travelling with a party of adults.

Is this type of holiday for you?

Not everyone will enjoy this type of holiday. While they can be a lot of fun and often gave great educational value, holidays off the beaten track can also be very tiring. Beneath are some questions to ask yourself if you are considering taking an adventurous holiday with your young family.

- Are you a 'home body' or happy to live without your home comforts?

- Are you and your children adaptable, or do you and they prefer routine?

- Do you like to plan everything or are you happy to encounter the unexpected?

- Are you happy for your children to take anti-malarial drugs and/or have extra vaccinations?

- What is your children's school's attitude to taking children out of school?

- Are your children fussy eaters?

- Does anyone in the family have specific medical requirements?

- What is your budget?

- Are you often anxious about your children's safety or generally quite relaxed?

■ Do you feel that travelling has educational value?

Thinking about these questions will help you decide if an adventurous holiday is for you and/or what kind of holiday you might want to take.

For example, if you would like to experience something very exotic but don't want to be without your home comforts a luxury safari might suit you well, assuming your budget will stretch to it. If you are happy without home comforts and your children's school is flexible about extended holidays, an extended backpacking trip could be for you.

Passports and visas

Check that all passports (including your children's) are up to date at least two months before your holiday. Bear in mind that for entry into some countries, you need at least six months remaining on your passport. Check if you will require a visa on the Foreign Office website and apply for it in good time.

Safaris

A safari can be an easy and safe way to experience the very exotic and will almost certainly be a holiday to remember for the whole family. The downside is that this type of holiday can be very expensive.

On luxury family safari holidays you will usually stay in a very comfortable game reserve and game drives will be organised for you. Alternatively, you may travel between several lodges and/or tents. The type of safari you will choose will depend on the ages and adventurousness of your children – make sure you ask lots of questions before booking so you know exactly what you are getting in to.

You may want to choose a safari which is specifically suitable for children and it is important to check the lower age limit as this varies greatly. Some companies will allow children as young as five on certain game drives and others provide childcare and animal-based activities at the lodge. Many will tailor-make a holiday especially for you.

'Our safari was an exceptional family holiday experience. Our son is eight and our daughter is and they both saw so much wildlife and learned a lot from the experienced guides.'

Lisa, who stayed at Governors' Camp on the Masai Mara.

For example, Sabi Sabi Game Lodge in South Africa has recently opened its 'Elefun Centre' where children aged four to 12 who don't want to go out on safari can learn about animals and go on nature walks. Heritage Hotels offer an Adventurers' Club at their lodges for children aged four to 12 with outdoor, nature and animal-based activities.

Most companies stress that there is no set youngest age for game drives as every child is different. To take part in a game drive a child should be able to sit still and quietly for a reasonable length of time. If yours are not yet at this stage, it might be best to wait a few years (when they would also probably better appreciate and remember the experience) or book a safari holiday with a childcare option.

Case study

Kavitha has taken her children on safari twice in India – the first time the youngest was just three years old:

'I had prepared the kids by telling them that they would only see deer and birds as I didn't want them to be disappointed if we didn't see lions and tigers as sightings are rare. But as it was we saw elephant, boar, birds and even glimpsed a tiger on our last day.

'My three year old was still at the stage where he got excited by small birds and deer so it wouldn't have really mattered if we hadn't seen the tiger anyway – but it was a bonus.

'It was tiring for them sitting still but they managed pretty well. The guides were very good, telling lots of interesting stories.'

'Backpacking isn't just for students and young people on gap years – it's perfectly possible to do it as a family.'

Backpacking

Backpacking isn't just for students and young people on gap years – it's perfectly possible to do it as a family.

If you have never this type of trip before, it will usually be best to keep your first trip short and not too far away while you see how you all get on without the comforts of home.

While you may well want to feel free and easy and be able to travel where you want, it can be helpful to book your first night's accommodation at the very least to give you an easy start to your trip.

You and your children may find your trip less tiring if you plan to stay in each place for a few days rather than moving on every day, but of course this depends on your preferences. If your budget allows, you may like to alternate cheap, basic places to stay with occasional hotels which are more luxurious with better facilities.

It is sometimes possible to buy a day pass to expensive hotels in some places to use to pool and enjoy a relaxing day – this may be particularly welcome in hot cities.

Once you have enjoyed a short, successful trip, this will give you a good idea of what does and doesn't work for you and your family – and you can plan a longer, more adventurous one for next time.

Case study

Becky on her short backpacking trip in Italy with her daughter Eve:

'I really enjoyed backpacking around Italy with Eve, she was one at the time and people absolutely loved her when we were out and about.

'The hostels were very accommodating and all I did was to make sure that the hostel offered private rooms before arriving, however, there were no cots, changing mats or baths which was difficult with a small baby. Also, because she wasn't a "person" when we stayed somewhere she didn't get a breakfast included like we did, but that was fine, I just bought fresh fruit for her breakfast instead.

'Although we did have to make some compromises and perhaps didn't do as much sightseeing as you could without a baby, it was still a great adventure!'

Case study

Jess has been backpacking with her children since they were babies, travelling around countries including Mexico and Vietnam.

'My husband Paul and I had done a lot of travelling before the children were born and we always knew that having children wasn't going to change that. I had always dreamt of having four seats on the bus!

'We haven't found that having the children with us on travels has affected what we do at all – other than we don't go out so much at night. We still tend to stay in budget accommodation, arrive without a plan and see where we end up. That's the way we've always done it and because the children are used to it, it doesn't seem to bother them at all.

'The journey is very much part of the experience for us – we are used to 28 hour bus journeys feeding the kids Frosties from a packet. That was very easy when they were tiny and fine now that they are seven and 11 – although I will admit to taking along their Nintendos! When they were about two or three it wasn't so easy and we tended to fly for very long journeys. We've tried "ordinary" family holidays but they're just not for us. We're hoping to go to China for our next trip.

'One tip I have for families is to stay in budget accommodation, even if you can afford mid-range, to get a real feel for the place you are visiting. It might sound odd but it tends to be the budget accommodation which will really put you in the centre of things.

'I think our trips are an amazing experience for the children – they are both very independent and confident and I'm sure being well-travelled has contributed to that.'

Jess's daughter Imani, now 11, has been backpacking with her parents for up to five weeks at a time since she was a baby. She says:

'I love that we never know what to expect – we can arrive somewhere and there's something amazing which we didn't expect. We ended up in a very horrible hotel room once in Mexico when we couldn't find anywhere else but it was only for one night so it was okay.'

Health and Safety

Before you go

Before you travel anywhere a little more unusual it is important to check for up-to-date advice about any dangers and also required vaccinations.

Your first port of call should be the Foreign Office website which will give you information about any particular current threats (e.g. terrorism) in any given country as well as recommended vaccinations.

Visit your GP at least eight weeks before travelling to find out about any necessary vaccinations. Depending on where you are going, these may include yellow fever, hepatitis A, typhoid, meningoccal meningitis and tetanus and polio.

It is important to do this well in advance as some vaccinations take several weeks to become effective. You may find you have to pay for some vaccinations or order them in advance. Your GP will advise.

'Make sure you have adequate travel insurance for the entire time you plan to be away.'

Make sure you have adequate travel insurance for the entire time you plan to be away.

A special word about malaria

Some parents have reservations about their children taking anti-malarial drugs because of potential side effects. If you are travelling to a malarial region, it is very important that your children are adequately protected. If you are not happy for your children to take anti-malarial drugs you should consider travelling only to places which are free of malaria. Malaria is a potentially fatal illness.

Even if you and your children have taken anti-malarials, it is still possible to get the disease. Use malaria nets at night, encourage your children to wear long trousers and sleeves and use a strong mosquito spray.

Every year around 2,000 British travellers return home with malaria. If you or your child shows symptoms of malaria, which are similar to those of flu, either while travelling or within one year of returning from a malarial region, seek immediate medical attention.

Food safety

The type of precautions you will need to take will depend to a degree on where you are travelling, but beneath are some general rules.

If you are travelling somewhere where it is unsafe to drink the water, remember that it is also vital you do not drink drinks with ice in them. You should also only eat fruit which you have peeled yourself and avoid salads or other foods which may have been washed. Remember to brush your teeth using bottled water.

It can only take a very small amount of contaminated water to make you or your children very ill. If your children are old enough, explain this to them. Make sure you always carry or have access to clean water to ensure your children do not become dehydrated.

You cannot always expect the same food hygiene standards to be followed as you are used to while you are travelling. Nonetheless, you should try to exercise the same common sense judgement as you would at home.

If an establishment looks dirty, avoid it. If you are worried about how food has been stored (perhaps if you are eating from a street stall), avoid it or at least stick to a well-cooked vegetarian option.

It can be useful to carry your own clean plastic plates and cutlery if you are planning to eat from street vendors. Ensure all food is cooked through and do not eat cooked food which has been stored next to raw meat.

If your children are very fussy eaters, try to find things which are almost familiar yet different. For example, noodles are like spaghetti, lassi is like a milkshake and kulfi like ice cream. Many children will try almost any meat if you tell them 'It's a bit like chicken'. Or try gentle bribery, for example, 'If you try this, you can have one of these sweets'.

Even if your children refuse to try new things you can usually find foods which are familiar, like rice, spaghetti bolognaise or pancakes, almost anywhere.

Travelling is a great time for you and your children to experiment with new tastes. It can be tempting to stick to 'safe' foods and establishments which you recognise, but with a little bit of care and common sense it is often possible to eat safely from very humble-looking places.

'It can only take a very small amount of contaminated water to make you or your children very ill.'

Travel first aid kit

You should take a small first aid kit with you just in case anyone gets a scrape or cut. Try to fit in:

Plasters and bandages.

- Safety pins.
- Cotton wool.
- Small scissors.
- Paracetamol and infant paracetamol.
- Rehydration powder.
- Clean syringes (depending on where you are travelling).
- Tweezers.
- Thermometer.
- Antiseptic wipes or cream.

'Find out about
your child's
school's attitude
to taking
trips during
term time.'

Extended trips

For some families, travelling during the school holidays simply isn't enough and they want to do more. This can be anything from a couple of months to several years.

If you are planning this kind of trip, it is important to think carefully about how it will affect your children's education. What stage of school are they at? How much school will they miss and how is it likely to affect them? It may depend not only on what age your children are but also how they manage at school. While some children will miss a few weeks or even months of school and catch up quickly, others may struggle.

Find out about your child's school's attitude to taking trips during term time. Some are very strict and you may find you return to find your child's place has been given away – especially if it is an over-subscribed school.

If you are planning to be away for several months you will have to think about how you are going to educate your children while you are away. While they will probably be gaining many useful and educational experiences, they will still need to keep up with their reading and maths so that they do not fall behind their peers.

It is legal to home school your child while travelling and you do not have to be a teacher to do so. For more information and resources on educating your children yourself visit www.home-schooling-uk.com.

Summing Up

- Backpacking isn't for everyone and it's important to make sure you're prepared for an 'off the beaten track' adventure – ask yourself if you're ready for this and if your children will enjoy themselves.

- Check all passports are up to date and research the visa requirements for your destination well in advance of leaving.

- A safari could be an easy and safe way for your family to experience an 'off the beaten track' holiday, the downside is that these type of holidays can be very expensive. If you choose to go on safari with your children, make sure you research the tour company and accommodation to make sure you know what you're getting in to.

- Backpacking can be done with children, whether it's for a short travelling break somewhere close by or an extended tour of somewhere very adventurous. However, take into consideration your children's ages, personalities and interests before planning a packed itinerary!

- Make sure you're aware of any vaccinations and medication required for the country you wish to travel to. Visit your GP at least eight weeks before you plan to travel. Be aware of the risks of malaria and even if you're taking anti-malarial medication take steps to avoid mosquito bites.

- Make sure you explain to your children that they shouldn't drink tap water and use common sense when choosing where to buy food from. If in doubt, stick to a well-cooked vegetarian option.

- For families taking a very extended travelling trip, you'll need to check with your child's school and possibly look into home schooling.

Chapter Eight

Skiing

Whatever age your children are, a holiday in the mountains can be great for the whole family.

When to start

Most ski schools will take children aged three and upwards as long as they are out of nappies during the daytime.

How will they learn?

Unless you are a very experienced skier, it is wise to book your child into lessons. Even if you ski very well, you may find your child accepts instruction better from a stranger.

Very small children (aged three to four or five) have short lessons (usually about one hour) in a protected 'snow garden' which is usually close to the resort centre rather than high on the mountain. It has a very shallow incline where children will first learn to walk in tiny skis and progress on to skiing a short distance through the enclosed garden – often through little arches painted to look like cartoon characters. Many snow gardens have a 'magic carpet' – a little conveyor belt to take the children to the top.

One-to-one lessons are also available – some instructors will take children as young as two on a private basis. Older children will start their lessons on a gentle nursery slope.

'Unless you are a very experienced skier, it is wise to book your children into lessons.'

You can find out about local ski schools through the individual resorts' websites. If you book a package holiday the tour operator may book a ski school for you. Family-specialist tour operators will usually take children to and from the ski school and often accompany them during lessons.

Will my children like it?

Every child is different. Chances are a physically active and adventurous three-year-old will love their introduction to skiing, but if your child is a timid, gentle character it might be better to wait until they are a few years older. Consider taking your child for their first ski trip in the spring when it will be warmer and there is less risk of them getting too cold.

If you feel your child is not ready for skiing, there are plenty of other activities to keep them happy in a ski resort. Almost every child enjoys sledging and building snowmen and most resorts have very good kids' clubs and nurseries for babies which will allow you some time on the slopes by yourself.

'Almost every child enjoys sledging and building snowmen.'

Package trips

There is a huge variety of operators offering ski package trips – including several which are aimed purely at families. Two excellent, but very different ones, are Club Med and Esprit which both provide ski lessons and childcare, but there are many others.

The main advantage of a package ski holiday is that everything is organised for you – your transfer from the airport to your lift pass and childcare to ski hire – if you so choose. This can take a lot of hassle out of both the organisation of your holiday and make your arrival day a lot easier.

Childcare

If your children are not old enough to ski, or are not competent skiers, you will probably want some childcare in order to make the most of your time on the slopes.

Packages which include childcare can make a ski holiday run much more smoothly for everyone. If you book carefully through a family-orientated operator you should be able to find accommodation where the childcare is in the same building. Another advantage is that the carers are more likely to speak English.

Many family-orientated companies offer children's high tea, baby facilities and food, children's clubs for older children, evening babysitting and nannies to accompany the children to their ski lessons. Make sure you are clear about which services are included in the basic cost of your holiday and which may attract a further fee.

Travelling independently

Some families prefer to travel independently to their ski holidays. Even if you usually prefer to travel this way, it is worth looking at both options as for skiing holidays, independent travel is not always cheaper once all the components are added up and is often less convenient.

In particular, transfers from airports to ski resorts can be expensive and may leave you with quite a long walk up a snow-covered road or path once you arrive. However, travelling independently can offer greater flexibility and independence than package options, especially for stays of less than one week.

'Some families prefer to travel independently to their ski holidays.'

Accommodation when travelling independently

Individual resorts' websites usually have comprehensive information about accommodation available in the resort and you can often book directly through the site. Catered chalet and self-catering accommodation can also be found through websites such as www.holidaylettings.co.uk and www.holiday-rentals.co.uk.

Childcare when travelling independently

Most large resorts will have a well-organised crèche and children's club which will run all day – you can find out about them and book through resorts' websites. However, it can be difficult to find much information about them beyond the basics before booking.

While the carers will probably be used to looking after children of different nationalities, they will not necessarily speak English, which some children (or even parents) may find upsetting.

Accommodation

There are three main types of accommodation available in ski resorts – hotels, catered chalets and self-catered apartments. Which type you choose will be down to your personal preferences which may change as your children get older.

'Most large resorts will have a well-organised crèche and children's club.'

Catered chalets

Catered chalets are a popular choice for ski holidays. They range from fairly small – sleeping as few as four or six people – to large 'chalet hotels' sleeping up to 40 or 50. Each chalet is looked after by a chalet girl (or boy) or, in larger chalets, a small team who will make you breakfast, afternoon tea and dinner and clean your room every day.

Some will offer extras, such as tea in bed in the morning or a packed lunch. Some are fairly basic while others are more luxurious with hot tubs or saunas. Family-orientated ones may offer children's high tea.

Everyone eats together as if at a dinner party so they work well if you like to meet new people – they also mean you can have a sociable evening without having to go out (or get a babysitter). All food and wine is usually included in the booking price.

The staff will have one night a week off when they will be happy to suggest and often book a restaurant for you. Family-orientated chalets will often also provide evening babysitting at extra cost – this is usually free on the staff night off.

Hotels

Larger resorts may offer a range of hotels from fairly basic to five-star luxury. Hotels will generally offer more flexible dining options than catered chalets and may suit people who would rather spend more time on their own as a family but without having to cater for themselves.

Some ski hotels also have excellent facilities for children – Kinder Hotels operating in Austria, Bavaria and Lower Tyrol offer everything from children's meals and full day care and all sorts of activities for children (some have wizard schools!) to miniature bathrobes for children.

Self-catering

Self-catering apartments and chalets again can be anything from fairly basic to very luxurious. They can be a good option for families who want their own space and prefer to set their own timetable for mealtimes. Self-catering can be much more cost-effective for parents who don't want to share a bedroom with their children. The downside, of course, is that you have to do your own cooking and cleaning.

Case study

Anne, has been on several skiing holidays with her children aged six and eight:

'We've been most years since they were babies. When they were very little we tended to stay in a catered chalet with a family-friendly company so that everything was organised for us, the childcare was on-site, the nannies were English-speaking and dinner was cooked for us in the evening.

'Now that the children are big enough to ski we travel independently and rent a self-catering apartment so we have more flexibility. We all enjoy the holidays greatly – my husband and I get some much-needed time to ourselves as a couple while the children are in ski lessons and we also get to spend quality time as a family in beautiful surroundings.'

What else should I consider when booking?

Skiing almost inevitably involves a degree of walking in cumbersome ski boots, carrying heavy skis and awkward poles. When you have children in tow, you want to minimise this as much as possible. Here are some tips and things to consider:

- Book 'ski-in, ski-out' accommodation or at the very least, accommodation which isn't far from the lifts and slopes.

- If you are planning to use childcare, ensure your accommodation is nearby.

- Do you want to share a room with your children or would you rather they have their own room?

- If you are flying, what is the transfer time to the resort?

- If you have a baby, can a travel cot and high chair be provided?

- If you would prefer your children to eat early, will this be possible?

- What other activities are there in the resort? Is there a pool or sledging area?

Equipment

The following items are essential for everyone – adults and children alike.

- Salopettes (waterproof, padded trousers) and a ski jacket or a ski suit. Ski suits can be warmer for children but make it more difficult to go to the toilet and they will probably get less year-round wear out of them.

- Ski gloves or mittens. Mittens are warmer but make doing up zips etc more difficult. Ordinary woollen gloves are not advised.

- Several pairs of ski socks.

- Thermal leggings and long-sleeved thermal T-shirts.

- A good thick jumper or fleece.

- Goggles or sunglasses. For children, and in bad weather, goggles are best.

- High-factor sun cream and lip balm – at altitude the sun is strong even in winter.

- A scarf or, ideally, a neck-warmer (which can't fall off like a scarf.)

- Ski gear can be expensive and children grow out of theirs quickly so it can make sense to borrow or buy second hand where you can. Alternatively, H&M and Blacks do reasonably-priced ranges.

- Buggies do not work well in deep snow. If you are travelling with a baby, consider taking a baby carrier.

Should we wear helmets?

Many ski schools insist that children in their care wear them and in Italy and lower Austria, it is obligatory for all children. In practice, most children wear helmets while skiing.

Death and serious head injury while skiing are very rare. However, helmet use for adults is increasing following some high-profile deaths from head injury while skiing, including Sonny Bono in 1998 and more recently, actress Natasha Richardson. Research is conflicting on whether helmets for adults make skiing safer and it is ultimately a personal choice. Helmets can be bought or hired from ski shops.

'Skis and boots can be easily hired in all ski resorts.'

What about skis and ski boots?

Skis and boots can be easily hired in all ski resorts. There is no need to pre-book but you may find you get a discount for doing so. You will find details of hire shops on the individual resorts' websites.

Snowboarding

Some children may prefer to learn to snowboard rather than ski. It is a totally different skill – more akin to skateboarding than skiing in some ways – and it is not necessary to be able to ski before learning to snowboard.

Many snowboarders claim it is easier to learn to snowboard than to ski, others say that the first few days can be more difficult as you tend to fall harder. Whether to learn to ski or snowboard is ultimately a personal choice and snowboarding lessons are available in most resorts. However, snowboarding is not usually recommended for children under the age of seven.

Lift passes

Lift passes can usually be bought from your tour operator if you are travelling on a package holiday or from the lift pass office in-resort. Some hotels and apartment building receptions also sell them.

Many resorts will have a small free lift for absolute beginners but beyond that, everyone will need a lift pass. Children under six are usually entitled to a free one, but you may need to supply proof of their age (such as a passport).

Larger resorts may offer several types of pass which allow you to access a smaller or greater area. Which one you choose will depend on your level of skiing and how much skiing you plan to do.

The cost of lift pass varies widely from resort to resort and this may be something you wish to consider when booking your holiday. Lift pass prices can generally be found on the individual resorts' websites.

For example – if all your family are total beginners, it might make sense to take your holiday in a small resort where the pass is cheaper. Resorts in Slovakia and Bulgaria are competitively priced and ideal for beginners, and in France, resorts in the Pyrenees are generally smaller and cheaper than those in the Alps.

If you are an expert skier, you may want to choose a resort with a wider range of pistes and a more expensive pass. Some resorts are linked to other resorts to create huge ski areas, such as Paradiski and Espace Killy in France and Portes du Soleil which straddles Switzerland and France.

Insurance

Winter sports insurance is vital. Every year around 140,000 skiers are injured in France alone. Medical costs abroad can be very expensive and in the unlikely event that you have to be helicoptered off the mountain, costs can run into thousands. Check that your travel insurance includes winter sports cover (you will usually have to ask for it specifically and pay extra) and check exactly what it covers. If you are skiing in Europe, make sure you take a current European Health Insurance Card (EHIC).

Summing Up

Skiing can be a great family holiday but it is vital to think about what you all want from your holiday and plan appropriately. If you and your partner want to ski as much as possible, good childcare will be high on your agenda. If one or both of you is going to be looking after a baby or small child much of the time, availability of other activities or a luxurious hotel might be more important to you. There is a huge range of skiing holidays available and with a little time and research you are bound to find one which suits your own particular needs.

Chapter Nine

Luxury, Cruises and Spas

Just because you have children doesn't mean you can no longer go to smart hotels or enjoy the finer things in life, if your budget allows.

Spas

Arguably, fewer people are in greater need of a relaxing spa break than parents of young children, and the owners and managers of spas have realised this. More and more spas, both in the UK and abroad, are including children in the spa experience.

Crèches

Some spas have crèches for children from as young as three months usually up to the age of around eight. As with all kids' clubs you should ask about the ratio of adults to children and about what kind of activities the children will be doing. See chapter 3 for more about crèches and kids' clubs.

At many spas you will need to book a crèche place in advance and sessions will often be limited to a few hours at a time – check when you book.

Spas which offer crèches and accommodation in the UK include Aquae Sulis at Luxury Family Hotel Group properties, Aqua Sana at Center Parcs and Celtic Manor in Wales. There are many more.

'Fewer people are in greater need of a relaxing spa break than parents of young children.'

Treatments for teens and tweens

Some spas now offer treatments for older children. Runnymede Hotel in Surrey offers a whole series of treatments aimed specifically at teens including a facial, massage, pedicure and make up lessons for 13 to 17-year-olds. The Serenity Spa at Seaham Hall, Country Durham also offers treatments for teenagers. The Vineyard at Stockcross offers a facial, manicure and pedicure for under-12s.

Mum-to-be treatments

Many spas, especially those aimed at families – offer special treatments for pregnant women. These tend to be very relaxing treatments focusing on the areas which tend to suffer during pregnancy and only use products which are safe for use during pregnancy.

'Some spas now offer treatments for older children.'

It is usually also possible to enjoy many mainstream treatments while pregnant but it is important to let your therapist know about your pregnancy in case the treatment needs to be modified.

Pregnant women are usually advised not to use saunas or steam rooms and to avoid very hot Jacuzzis. If in doubt, check with your GP or midwife before you go.

Children in common areas

Some spas will allow children into pools at certain times, others will also allow them to use sauna and steam room areas (usually under parental supervision).

Check what the policy of the spa is before you book. It may be that you would prefer your children to be able to use the pool with you – although bear in mind that this will mean that other people's children will probably be there too!

If you are after peace and quiet, you may prefer a spa where any children remain in a crèche.

Swimwear

In the UK, spa users are generally expected to wear swimwear. Other countries vary – in some (such as Germany and Austria) it is more common for spa users to be naked.

In some family-friendly spas on days when children are allowed in adults are asked to cover up, but this is not always the case. If you are uncomfortable with nudity, check in advance.

Other spas to take your children to

There are many spas around the world with children's facilities – here are just a few:

- Aquacity Poprad, Slovakia – a myriad of naturally-heated thermal pools including one with a swim-up bar. It also offers massages and cryotherapy – a treatment which involves spending minutes in a chamber at -120°C! For children there is a water park and a supervised playroom.

- Out of the Blue, Agia Pelagia, Heraklion, Greece – while you enjoy a chocolate or honey massage at the Euphoria Spa, your children can have the time of their lives at the resort's very own Minoan Amusement Park.

- Hotel Schwarz, Tyrol, Austria – a full programme of kids' activities including a petting zoo, magic lessons, swimming lessons and a youth theatre. The spa has a huge array of saunas and steam rooms including an outdoor sauna and traditional Turkish hammam – plus beauty treatments and even plastic surgery.

- Azia Resort, Paphos, Cyprus – mothers and daughters can sit side by side for manicures with extra flowers and sparkles for the little girls or parents can watch through a glass wall as their children have shoulder massages in a special glass-walled area of the spa.

- La Manga Resort, Murcia, Spain – a huge resort covering an area the size of Monaco. As well as a large spa there are also three golf courses, five swimming pools and the option to go go-karting, quad-biking, kayaking or kite surfing. There is a kids' club for younger children while older children can enjoy a similar range of activities.

Anne says: 'I love going to spas with my kids – it is absolutely my favourite thing. My husband and I get to have a couple of hours off enjoying the steam rooms while the kids are entertained and then afterwards, if it's one where the children are allowed in the pool, we all go swimming. Everyone's happy!'

Cruises

Cruises may not seem an obvious choice for a family holiday, but they come in many different forms and many are ideal for children.

Cost

Cruises can vary from fairly basic to extremely luxurious and the price will reflect the level of luxury you choose, as well as your destination. If you choose a cruise which starts from a destination you need to fly to, this will be more expensive than a cruise which starts in the UK.

'People tend to either love or hate cruises.'

The booking price may sometimes seem expensive but it is worth checking exactly what is included. Most cruises will include all meals, some will include drinks and excursions while for others these will cost extra. Make sure you read the small print.

Some cruise lines will also add on tips. These should be optional and you can ask for them to be removed but in most cases you will want to budget for them.

People tend to either love or hate cruises. Beneath are some advantages and disadvantages.

Advantages

- You get to visit several places easily.
- Everything is arranged for you.
- A cruise provides a safe, enclosed environment for children. Some will even arrange children's activities.

Disadvantages

- While there are usually various options for activities and excursions, to a large degree you have to follow the itinerary.

- You can feel a bit claustrophobic if you don't like being in a crowd.

- Limited dining options (although larger ships will have several restaurants).

Cruises suitable for children

- Carnival Cruises carried 600,000 children in 2008, roughly half of all children cruising with American companies. They operate cruises to 60 destinations including Alaska, Hawaii, Bermuda, Panama Canal and Europe. Kids' activities are led by trained counsellors and are available for ages two to 17 on 'Fun Ships' and parents are given beepers in case they are needed. Carnival also offers babysitting in a 'slumber party' atmosphere, supervised children's dining and excursions, 24-hour pizza and ice cream and rooms are larger than normal accommodating up to five people. Interconnecting cabins are also available. All ships have corkscrew water sides and one Fun Ship, *Carnival Dream*, boasts a water park with 303m four-deck water slide – the longest in cruising.

- Royal Caribbean International Cruises – with over 100 ports of call, onboard entertainment includes climbing walls, water flumes and surf simulators – there are also kids' clubs for all ages, interconnecting rooms and suites which will accommodate families of up to 16. At 'My Family Time Dining' children are served quickly and you can even have the Youth Team take your children to the kids' club after they have finished eating while you finish your own meal. During morning 'Stroll & Roll' sessions the jogging track is reserved for parents with buggies. Babysitting is available and there is even a board game menu to choose from.

- Disney Cruises – Disney cruises offer Disney-themed kids' entertainment as well as Broadway-quality original Disney musicals which can't be seen anywhere else, deck parties for the whole family with fireworks and most cruises include a stop at the Disney Island Paradise. Destinations include Alaska, Bahamas, Panama Canal and Transatlantic.

'Research the destinations you are going to visit to help you make the most of them.'

Linda.

Linda's top tips for a successful family cruise

- Cruising is a wonderful way to spend a holiday, but there is so much to see and do, you may be spoilt for choice.

- Make sure your cruise is genuinely family-friendly – just because children can go, it doesn't mean they are going to enjoy it. Look closely at the marketing material. Are children pictured having a great time or are all the images of adults sipping cocktails and gazing into each others' eyes?

- Plan well ahead – ask all family members for their input so that they know there'll be plenty of chances to do what they want, and minimise the chances of bickering.

- Research the destinations you will visit to help you make the most of them. With a fleeting stay in some places, prior knowledge is power.

- Get to know your ship before you set foot on it. Check with your company to see how much information they can provide – some offer DVDs of their ships or virtual tours on their websites. Alternatively, you can find out more from other people's stays on YouTube.

- Check out the staterooms or cabins – what are the arrangements for children's sleeping? Are cots available and is there a fee to rent one during the day?

- Make sure you are clear about dining times and how these fit with your family. Is there an earlier sitting you can take advantage of? Choose an option that suits a time slot near to when your children usually eat so routines aren't overly disrupted – even on holiday, this can lead to stress.

- Think about money. While you can enjoy not having to spend cash onboard, thanks to the all-inclusive nature of cruising and supplying credit or debit card details at the start of your stay for gifts and drinks, the places you visit may have different currencies. Get the best exchange rate you can for each of your destinations.

Luxury

While, as a general rule, parents shouldn't feel they have to be limited to specifically 'family-friendly' resorts, luxury holidays are one type of holiday where you may prefer to choose one with some child-friendly elements. You and your family may feel uncomfortable in a hotel crammed with honeymooners or packed with delicate ornaments and exquisite fabrics!

Remember that most children are not going to be impressed by luxury. As long as they are comfortable and happy, one hotel room will be much like another to them – they are more likely to be interested in a wardrobe door with a mirror than 400-count Egyptian cotton sheets.

There are plenty of luxurious hotels and resorts both in the UK and abroad which welcome children. In the UK, the Luxury Family Hotel Group offers a country house ambiance in small hotels with beautiful grounds along with crèches and children's high tea.

There are very many places both short haul and long haul which offer great luxury and are also child-friendly, from five star hotels in Dubai to 'blue water' destinations in the Maldives. For some ideas visit www.childfriendly.co.uk which is searchable by country, date and type of holiday – including luxury, or www.babygoes2.co.uk.

'Most children are not going to be impressed by luxury. As long as they are comfortable and happy, one hotel room will be much like another to them.'

Eating out

Whether you are booking a luxury holiday or just fancy a 'posh night out' while you are on a camping trip, it can be fun to take your children to a smart restaurant once in a while if your budget stretches to it.

Many children enjoy getting specially dressed up and being allowed to stay up late. Unless your children are very fussy, you will usually find something on the menu which will suit them, such as steak or a simple pasta dish.

Upmarket restaurants do not usually offer children's menus (although there are exceptions) but will usually be happy to make a dish without sauces, split one meal between two children or serve a smaller portion.

Take along small notepads and pens so your children can draw or scribble while they are waiting for food or perhaps offer a small prize if your children can behave well and eat all their food; even the bits which look 'strange'.

'Unless your children are very fussy, you will usually find something on the menu which will suit them, such as steak or a simple pasta dish.'

Need2Know

Summing Up

Sometimes you might want to push the boat out and enjoy an extra special holiday as a family. Just as with any other type of holiday, there is no reason not to do this as long as you plan ahead and pick the right destination. Go on, spoil yourself!

Chapter Ten

Holidays on a Budget

Sometimes you may find you have next to nothing left in the kitty for a holiday, but this doesn't mean you have to go entirely without. This chapter covers some ideas for holidays which won't break the bank.

Home swaps

There are many websites available which allow you to swap your house with another family for anything from a few days to several months.

You don't have to live in a mansion or necessarily live in a particularly touristy area to be able to swap your house. If you want to keep your budget right down you can swap with another family in the UK to minimise travel costs.

Alternatively, you can swap with someone on the other side of the world. Your town may not seem very exciting to you as a holiday destination but someone who lives somewhere very different may disagree.

'You don't have to live in a mansion or necessarily live in a particularly touristy area to be able to swap your house.'

What are the advantages?

Staying in someone's home rather than in a hotel or holiday apartment can be a really good way of getting to know somewhere almost as a member of the community rather than simply as a holidaymaker.

You will have all the comforts of home – a kitchen, separate bedroom for the children and if you choose carefully, perhaps even some toys.

There is no need to clear out your home for a swap as if you were renting it, although it is wise to pack away any valuable items and clear some space so your incoming family have somewhere to put their personal items.

How does it work?

You pay a small fee to sign up to a website – some are detailed in the help list. You can usually browse these sites free of charge so have a look first to see if they have the type of properties you are looking for in the kind of places you want to go.

Once you have decided which site would suit you best, you pay a fee (usually around £30 per year) and enter details and photos about your house, as well as details about places you would consider swaps with and possible dates. Then you sit back and wait for offers, or contact owners of properties you would be interested in swapping with.

Obviously if you live in a picturesque cottage in the Lake District or similar, it is likely that you will receive more offers than if you live somewhere less touristy. But many house swappers are doing so to visit friends and family or simply to have a base in the UK while they travel around so it can work for anyone.

'Home swapping is a brilliant way to travel, especially for families.'

Sarah.

It helps if you are reasonably flexible about when and where you would like to holiday. If you aim to swap with a family with similar-aged children, you should find that the house will be safe for them, any equipment you need (e.g. high chairs and cots) will be there and there will probably be some age-appropriate toys and games.

Some swappers may also be happy to swap their car or look after your pets. It's all about negotiating politely and being as flexible as possible.

Home swap tips

- Draft your advert carefully – include details of your home, facilities, family and local area. Be flexible with your dates and preferred destinations.

- Make sure you include good photographs, or even better, create a website using a free and easy to use site maker such as www.moonfruit.com.

- Take the initiative and write to several prospective exchangers rather than simply waiting for offers. Be friendly and address them personally.

- Always reply to an offer even if you do not want to take it up.

Case study

Sarah has taken two home swap holidays with her husband and two boys:

'Our first swap was with a French-Canadian family who had children of a similar age to ours – four and seven at the time – they lived in a house with a park and swimming pool just over the road.

'I was quite worried about booking the flight as there wouldn't have been any legal protection if they had pulled out, so we arranged to book our flights at the same time and email each other the confirmation details.

'We swapped cars too – when you arrive in a strange country with two children it's brilliant to have a car waiting for you.

'We found it so relaxing to be in a home, with all the accessories there. If it was a rainy day we could kick back and relax – we didn't feel pressurised to get out at a certain time. We could cook for ourselves or go to a local restaurant and it was great to know that someone was in our house too – my parents have been burgled three times while they have been away.

'Last year we went to Sweden and had a fantastic holiday which cost a total of £300 for all four of us! The flights cost £30 through Ryanair's £1 deal and we hardly spent anything while there. We stayed in Stockholm but the Swedes had a second house at the beach which we could use for free.

'I always cook a meal for the visiting family and leave a small gift for the children and then another gift to say thank you when we leave. Home swapping is a brilliant way to travel, especially for families.'

'Last year we went to Sweden and had a fantastic holiday which cost a total of £300 for all four of us!'

Sarah.

- Communicate throughout and be honest about what you have to offer. If you want to include an extra guest or pet, ask in advance. Keep in regular contact to create mutual trust.

- Once you have confirmed, discuss formalities. Ask questions and offer information. Agree who will pay phone and utility bills and for any repairs or breakages. Most sites have an agreement form you can download – you may like to use one to avoid any misunderstandings.

- Let your house insurance and, if applicable, car insurance companies know about your planned swap.

- Prepare a 'Home Book' with practical information about where to find the fusebox and stopcock, operate the TV and appliances, where to leave the bins on which day etc. Leave a list of useful numbers and some up-to-date tourist information maps and leaflets.

- Clean thoroughly. Make space in cupboards and drawers for your incoming family to put their possessions.

- Try to meet your guests if possible. If not, leave a welcome letter and perhaps a bottle of wine.

- When leaving, ensure you have agreed what to do with keys and used linen. Don't forget to leave a thank you letter.

Tips provided by John and Marilyn, Home Base Holidays Newsletter.

Staycations

'Almost anywhere, town or country, has tourist attractions.'

The term 'staycation' has been used a lot during the credit crunch to describe holidays in the UK. But to save even more money you can take it a step further and stay at home – but try to see your area like a tourist.

- Almost anywhere, town or country, has tourist attractions and however long you have lived where you are, it is unlikely you have visited them all.

- Plan a little. Try to get as many household chores out of the way as possible and take time off work.

- If your local town has a tourist office, go along and see what's on. If not, try the Internet – NetMums has regional sites with details of things to do with little ones. Your local library will also have some suggestions.

- Make an itinerary and plan your days so that you don't simply stay at home wondering what to do or waste half the day while you decide. Do all those things which you see tourists do but have never done – perhaps take an open-top bus tour if there is one available or visit the local petting zoo.

- If the weather is good, have a picnic in the garden or your local park. Go for a bike ride. Visit local museums – many, even small ones, offer children's activities. You'll probably be surprised how much there is you can do in your local area.

Other ways to save

Airmiles

There are many ways to collect Airmiles – these include using supermarket loyalty cards, special Airmiles credit cards, shopping online, recycling mobile phones, taking holidays and travelling and by collecting newspaper tokens.

In a nutshell, the more Airmiles you earn the longer flight you can take for free. Airmiles can also be 'spent' on hotels, package holidays and family days out and the beauty of them is that you can earn them while spending money you would be spending anyway.

Some families put their entire day-to-day spending on an Airmiles credit card in order to maximise their benefits. If you plan to do this, ensure you pay off your credit card balance in full to avoid attracting any interest payments.

Airline credit cards

Some airlines offer free flights with their own-brand credit cards. Some will offer free flights as soon as you sign up, others offer flights when you spend a certain amount of money.

Offers change regularly and the terms and conditions can sometimes make booking free flights quite inflexible so it is important to read them closely. In particular pay attention to whether the free flights include the taxes and charges which is often the largest part of the fare on budget flights.

Again, if you are using a credit card it is important to pay off the balance in full at the end of each month to avoid interest charges. For the latest offers, visit www.moneysavingexpert.com.

'Some airlines offer free flights with their own-brand credit cards.'

Cheap flights

Budget airlines regularly hold sales when flights can be bought for as little as £1. Sign up for email alerts with airlines such as Ryanair and easyJet so that you are told in advance when these sales are – you can make huge savings. But do read the small print – sometimes the advertised fares will not include taxes and other charges, such as booking fees.

Newspaper tokens and other vouchers

Several times a year several newspapers run promotions offering cut-price family holidays to holiday parks in the UK and all over Europe – from around £15 per person in the summer holidays and from £9.50 at other times of the year. Tokens are printed in the paper which must be submitted with your application. *The Sun* promotion is probably the best known but similar promotions are also run by *The Express*, *Mail* and *Star*.

'Budget airlines regularly hold sales when flights can be bought for as little as £1.'

Terms and conditions vary from year to year, but generally you can choose the area you want to go to and list your preferred parks and dates. When budgeting, it is important to look out for extras – for example there will often be a daily service charge or you may be charged for linen hire or entertainment.

The promotions are very popular so it is wise to get your tokens and form in as early as possible to increase the likelihood of getting your preferred dates and location.

Case study

Kerry used tokens from *The Sun* to take a holiday at a Haven holiday park:

'We paid about £68 for three nights, including compulsory service charges and optional service charges. We couldn't have afforded to go away for the weekend by any other method.

'We mainly went out and did our own beach and heritage type stuff, but the entertainment passes were a godsend on the day it rained. The people there were just exactly like us – families with young kids who wanted a cheap break and couldn't afford to go elsewhere.'

Need2Know

As well as using vouchers to pay for your holiday, it is also worth collecting vouchers to use for outings and meals while you are away on holiday.

Case study

Mother of three, Camilla, regularly saves money by collecting vouchers:

'I must admit I am a voucher fiend, but when you have three kids and with the price of admission to things, I think you have to be.

'I largely rely on Tesco Clubcard vouchers and have previously traded them in for vouchers to zoos, wildlife parks, castle visits, theme parks, museums and exhibitions.

'I also use their vouchers for meals at Pizza Express. One holiday, I saved over £250 on days out and meals. I also cut out 2-4-1 vouchers from cereal/ cake boxes for places like Legoland which saves us a ridiculous amount of money per visit.

'It's not about being cheap, it's about being thrifty, getting my kids a great day out at the best price and saving the money to use for something else, like paying for the holiday!'

> 'I must admit I am a voucher fiend but when you have three kids and with the price of admission to things, I think you have to be.'
>
> Camilla.

Cheap hotels and hostels

Hostels can be variable – some can be very good, some grotty. Many offer family rooms. Have a look at www.hostelbookers.com and www.hostelworld.com both of which offer user ratings.

Hostelbookers' PR executive Giovanna Gentile said: 'Over the past few years hostels have undergone a makeover and nowadays it is not uncommon to find hostels that represent the perfect choice for families who love travelling. Hostels can have a great atmosphere for families and keep costs down in many ways. The rate for a family room in a hostel will be a lot cheaper than in a hotel and most have a kitchen for all of their guests to use, meaning you can cook up meals and snacks and not have to dine out all the time. Not all hostels are suitable for families though – look out for one with family rooms and check it has the facilities you need on a website like www.hostelbookers.com before you book.'

For hotels at bargain prices, consider a 'secret hotel' on www.lastminute.com. The site will give you details about the location and facilities of the hotel as well as how many stars it has but won't reveal the identity of the hotel until you have booked and paid.

However, if you cut and paste the description into a search engine, it is usually possible to guess which hotel you are booking.

'Hostels can be variable – some can be very good, some grotty.'

Case study

Mother of two, Heidi, on staying in her first hostel:

'We stayed at a Letterfrack Lodge hostel in Connemara, County Galway in Ireland (www.letterfracklodge.com) for one night at the end of a two week camping holiday in Ireland. It had never occurred to me to stay in a hostel with children before (aged three and five) – I thought of them as places for backpackers. But the sight of a couple with a very young baby in the garden of this place as we drove in put us at ease. That night we all went out for a walk and a pint of Guinness and then put our boys to bed and made dinner in the communal kitchen and ate it in the dining room. Very civilised!

'I was very aware that the children were alone in our room, but I could hear them from the kitchen and actually felt they were very safe and they must have felt very at ease as they went straight to sleep. Our room had an ensuite shower room and toilet and the whole place was utterly spotless. It made me realise that hostelling could provide an affordable way to travel about and see some interesting parts of the world, and that it's entirely possible to do that with children.'

Convents and monasteries

Many convents and monasteries rent out rooms to families at very reasonable rates with no religious participation needed. The *Good Night and God Bless* range of books is excellent for finding suitable places or Google searches such as 'Convent stays' or 'Monastery stays' along with your chosen destination.

Colleges and universities

Many colleges and universities offer accommodation in halls of residence during holidays while their students are away. Flats are available so they can be suitable for families and can be very good value. Visit www.budgetstayuk.com.

Holiday saving tips from MoneySavingExpert.com

- Avoid debit cards – the worst cards for spending abroad can be some debit cards rather than credit cards, unless you don't pay off the credit card in full at the end of the month. Some cards give poor exchange rates and charge for cash withdrawals overseas and charge a fee of up to £1.50 every time you spend. Thus you can buy something for £3 worth of euros or dollars and end up paying £4.50 for it. Check what your card charges for overseas transactions before you leave.

- Carry a specialist overseas card – Almost every credit or debit card adds a 3% 'load' to the exchange rate when you spend abroad, so spend £100 worth of Euros and it'll cost you £103 (and this isn't shown on your statement). Some specialist credit cards don't add this 'load', giving you near perfect exchange rates, so get one just for spending abroad, but do ensure you repay it in full to reduce interest. These cards can save you £100s a year on holiday costs – for the latest on the best specialist overseas card for you go to www.moneysavingexpert.com/travelcards.

- Never pay in pounds – if a retailer overseas offers to let you pay in pounds, reject it. It's called dynamic currency exchange, and is common in Spain. It means that the shop will be doing the currency conversion; and if you don't know the rate it's usually worse than your card. That's especially true if you have one of the travel specialist cards.

- Get annual travel insurance if you trip away three times or more in a year – trip away three times or more in a year and an annual policy that covers the whole year's trips is usually cheapest, though if one of the trips is to the USA, it can be worth it if you do just one other trip. Bear in mind though, if you get an annual family policy, it may only cover you if all the family travel together and not if one goes independently. However, usually if you call and notify them of this, they do then allow it. Annual policies are available for as little as £15 for a year's travel in Europe for an individual or £25 for a family – full info on the latest at www.moneysavingexpert.com/travelinsurance.

- Car hire can be cheaper than a cab – booking ahead can often get you car hire at a fraction of the price, perhaps £10 a day rather than £50 or £60 once you are there. This can work out well, for example, between Malaga airport and Marbella in Spain, a taxi will cost you 50 Euros each way, yet cars can often be hired for less. So you could get a week's worth of trips for the cost of one taxi journey. To find the cheapest use comparison sites like sites like www.kayak.co.uk or www.carrentals.co.uk.

- Check out currency exchange rates – the worst place to get your travel money is at the airport or ferry port, because rates are inflated for captive customers. Even if you order cash online to be picked up at the airport, you will often get a better rate. Use an online comparison on www.travelmoneymax.com, which lists every currency. The savings you can make can be huge.

- Halve the cost of airport parking – airport parking is never cheap, so, if possible, avoid. Yet, if you need it, slash the cost by reserving as early as possible for the cheapest rates. Many providers will let you cancel with no charge if your plans change. To find the cheapest both on and off-site parking try comparison sites like www.aph.com and www.holidayextras.co.uk. Also, consider booking a night in an airport hotel, as they often offer a week's parking with a night's stay, which is occasionally cheaper than parking alone elsewhere. It can also make catching an early flight easier.

- Haggle to cut up to 15% off late package deals – if you've not booked yet, while DIY holidays are all the vogue, don't discount old-fashioned packages. Know what you're doing and they can be super cheap. Always remember holidays are created by tour operators and flogged by travel agents, so identical vacation packages are on offer at many agents. This means once you know where you want to go, the challenge is find who'll sell it to you cheapest. The best way is to simply telephone rival travel agents, including those who advertise in paper travel sections and see if they'll beat the price. Keep going until no one will – this can smash down the cost by a further 15%.

Need2Know

Summing Up

There is no denying that holidays can be very expensive, but whatever your budget, with a little planning and flexibility, it is possible to have a very enjoyable holiday for very little outlay.

Chapter Eleven

When Things Go Wrong

The vast majority of holidays pass happily without any major problems. However, it is important to be prepared in case you encounter problems so that you are better able to deal with anything which may arise.

Before you go

There are several things you can do while booking and before you leave for your holiday to prevent problems.

EHIC

If you are travelling in Europe, ensure the whole family has an up-to-date EHIC card, which entitles you to the same treatment as a resident of the country in which you are travelling. It is important to note that this does not always mean treatment will be free – this varies from country to country.

Insurance

It is vital to have good travel insurance. Even if you are covered by the EHIC, you need travel insurance to top up any medical costs not covered and potentially for booking extra travel and accommodation if a member of your family is taken ill and cannot travel.

According to research by www.bimuno.com, one in five Brits have had an accident while abroad and 27% have had to visit a doctor, hopefully nothing like this will happen on your holiday but it's important to be covered just in case it does.

'If you are travelling in Europe, ensure the whole family has an up to date EHIC card'

Travel insurance will also protect you in case of lost baggage and sometimes if you have to cancel your holiday. You can compare policies and features at www.moneysupermarket.com.

ABTA and ATOL

If you are booking through a tour operator, make sure they are ABTA or ATOL bonded. This way, if the company goes bust, you will get your money back.

Credit cards

'Pay for your holiday on a credit card, especially if you are booking independently.'

Pay for your holiday on a credit card, especially if you are booking independently, because you will not be covered by the ABTA or ATOL protection. With credit cards, any item costing over £100 and less than £30,000 will be covered by your credit card company under section 75 of the Consumer Credit Act. Therefore, if anything goes wrong, such as the company going into liquidation, your purchase is protected.

Passports, visas and vaccinations

Check that everyone's passport is up to date and you have any visas and vaccinations that you need. Remember that for entry into some countries your passport must have at least six months left before expiry. Visit the Foreign Office website for more information.

Email yourself

Scan your passports and any other important documents before you go and email them to yourself at an address which can be accessed from anywhere, such as a hotmail address. If you lose them, having a copy could be very useful. Otherwise photocopies should be carried separately with you, and another set left with a friend or relative in the UK.

Pack the brochure

Take the brochure, or at least the relevant pages, with you. It is easier to complain about a lack of a promised high chair or children's pool if you can point out the promises made in the brochure rather than relying on your memory.

Travel

If your plane is delayed by more than two hours you are entitled to free refreshments and, if necessary, overnight accommodation and phone calls. If your flight is cancelled you are entitled to compensation unless it was for reasons beyond the airline's control – but they must always give you a refund or a new flight.

To apply for compensation you should contact your tour operator or airline.

Accommodation

If you are unhappy with your accommodation, don't suffer in silence – speak up! If you have booked a package holiday your first port of call should be your holiday rep, who will usually have an appointed 'office hour' each day when he or she will be in a pre-arranged place. If you are travelling independently, ask to speak to the hotel manager.

Don't get angry or shout. Explain why you are unhappy with your room and suggest what could be done to rectify it. But be realistic. Complaints about cleanliness or safety are almost always valid (e.g. a dangerous balcony or if you have concerns about the plug sockets) but complaining simply because you 'don't like the room' is not usually going to win you much sympathy. If it is genuinely not as described in the brochure, point this out politely.

If the rep seems unwilling to help, ask to speak to their superior.

'If you are unhappy with your accommodation, don't suffer in silence.'

If your problem isn't resolved

Some problems will not be easily resolved – perhaps if the resort is too full and it is impossible to move you to a different room, or you are being disturbed by local building work.

Make notes about who you have spoken to about your complaint and what was said. Take pictures or video film illustrating the problem. Let your rep know that you will be making a formal complaint.

When you return, contact the customer service department of your holiday company and explain why you were unhappy. Send notes and pictures along with your complaint. Sample letters are available at www.which.co.uk.

ABTA guidelines dictate that the company must respond within 28 days. If you are unhappy about the response, write a 'final letter before action' (again see www.which.co.uk) stating that you will take the complaint to ABTA.

'Make notes about who you have spoken to about your complaint and what was said.'

If ABTA are unable to help, they also offer arbitration and mediation services. If this fails, your last resort is the Small Claims Court – see the help list for details.

Illness and injury

When you arrive at your destination, find out how you would contact a doctor or hospital in an emergency so that you are prepared. Take a simple first aid kit with you (see chapter 7) and painkillers for yourself and the children so you don't have to worry about finding a pharmacy and looking for medicines in unfamiliar surroundings and packaging for minor ailments.

If someone gets ill or injured, try not to panic. Things can often seem worse than they are when you are in a strange place – try to focus on how you would deal with the problem at home and act accordingly.

If you are on a package holiday, ask the rep to help you. Get them to accompany you to the hospital or doctor as they will speak the local language.

Contact your insurance company as soon as possible and find out what your options are if you need to extend your stay or rebook travel. Keep receipts for any medical treatment you pay for, including transport to and from appointments.

Lost or stolen goods

As far as you can, leave valuables at home and don't carry more cash than you need to when out and about. If your accommodation has a safe, use it for passports, jewellery and cash.

If you are planning to travel with valuables, check the small print of your travel insurance as the maximum payout on valuable items can be fairly low.

If something is stolen, even if you feel there is little chance of it being recovered, make sure you report it to the police or at the very least, a lost property office if you intend to claim for it on your insurance. Make sure you receive some kind of documentation.

Arrest and more serious problems

In the unlikely event that something very serious happens, such as someone being detained in prison unfairly, contact the local British Embassy. Embassies can be found through the Foreign Office website.

Summing Up

Most holidays go off without a hitch and even if you do encounter problems, most can be resolved without ruining your holiday. However, if you genuinely believe that your holiday did not live up to its promises, don't suffer in silence – speak up and seek compensation.

- Book with an ATOL or ABTA bonded agent.
- Pay with your credit card so you're protected by the Consumer Credit Act.
- Check about passports, visas and vaccinations well before you go.
- If travelling in Europe, pack an EHIC and ensure you have adequate travel insurance.
- Scan any important documents and email them to yourself.
- Take the brochure with you.
- If you are unhappy, speak up.
- If you are not satisfied, follow up your complaint when you get home.

Help List

Passports, visas and travel information

European Health Insurance Card (EHIC)

www.ehic.org.uk

Apply online for an EHIC which entitles you to the same treatment as a resident of the country in which you are travelling.

Foreign Office

www.fco.gov.uk

Check the Foreign Office for the latest information about visas, vaccinations, and which countries are considered dangerous.

Identity and Passport Service

www.ips.gov.uk

All you need to know about how to apply for a passport.

Weather

www.weather.co.uk

Check what the weather is like at your destination and also what it is like at different times of year.

Child-friendly holidays

Baby-friendly Boltholes

www.babyfriendlyboltholes.co.uk

Child-friendly accommodation, from stylish hotels to self-catering, in the UK and worldwide.

Baby Goes 2

www.babygoes2.com
Very useful family travel resource with destination and resort guides as well general tips.

Child friendly

www.childfriendly.co.uk
Searchable site for a wide variety of holidays.

Club Med

Tel: 08453 670 670
www.clubmed.co.uk
Wide variety of child-friendly holidays all over the world.

EspritSki

Tel: 01252 618 300
www.espritski.com
A specialist in family ski holidays.

Kinder Hotels

www.kinderhotels.com
Child-friendly hotels in Germany, Austria and Switzerland.

Luxury Family Hotel Group

www.luxuryfamilyhotels.co.uk
Child-friendly luxurious hotels in the UK.

Tots to Travel

Tel: 0845 269 4126
www.totstotravel.co.uk
Child-friendly self-catering accommodation in the UK and Europe.

Home swapping

Home Exchange

www.homeexchange.com
A home swap website where you can include details of your own home and where you'd like to go on holiday. There is a monthly fee.

Home Base Holidays

Tel: 020 8886 8752
www.homebase-hols.com
Home exchange website, there is a reasonable yearly fee.

Safaris

Heritage Hotels

www.heritage-eastafrica.com
Heritage Hotels provide 'beach and bush' adventure holidays in East Africa, they have good provisions for children and teens.

Sabi Sabi Game Lodge

www.sabisabi.com
Sabi Sabi Game Lodge offer child-friendly safari experiences.

Single parents

H.E.L.P Holidays

25 Brook Street, Hemswell, Gainsborough, DN21 5UJ
Tel: 01427 668717
www.helphols.co.uk
Charity which arranges low-cost holidays for lone parents, prisoners' wives and forces' wives whose husbands are abroad.

Single Parents on Holiday

Tel: 0871 500 4053

www.singleparentsonholiday.co.uk

Escorted tours for single parents with accommodation solely in four-star hotels.

Single Parent Travel Club

www.sptc.org.uk

A site which puts you in touch with other single parent families who want to go on holiday for a small joining fee.

Small Families

Tel: 0845 9000 895

www.smallfamilies.co.uk

The UK's largest specialist tour operator of escorted holidays abroad and UK weekend breaks for single parent families.

Theme parks

Butlins

Tel: 0845 070 4734

www.butlins.com

Butlins' three sites around the UK have been revamped over the recent years to try to shed its 'Hi-de-Hi' image and offers entertainment for the whole family.

Disneyland

http://disneyland.disney.go.com

Disneyland has sites in America, France and Hong Kong. Great rides and fantastic parades.

Gulliver's World

www.gulliversfun.co.uk

Theme parks especially for children aged two to 13, so ideal for little ones. Three parks around the UK – it is possible to camp at one.

PortAventura

Tel: 0800 696540

www.portaventura.co.uk

PortAventura is near Barcelona, has its own enormous water park and is on the coast. Ideal for a little bit of everything, especially in the hotter months.

Wunderland

www.wunderlandkalkar.eu

A theme park in Germany built in a disused nuclear power station complete with rides inside the old cooling tower. As much ice cream and chips as you can eat is included in the entry price.

Camping, caravans, mobile homes and lodges

Canvas Holidays

Tel: 0845 268 0827

www.canvasholidays.co.uk

Family camping holidays in Europe.

Cool Camping

www.coolcamping.co.uk

Independent campsites in the UK and abroad.

Eurocamp

Tel: 0844 406 0402

www.eurocamp.co.uk

Family camping holidays in Europe and America.

go4awalk.co.uk

www.go4awalk.co.uk

Advice about free camping and walking in the UK.

Free Campsites

www.freecampsites.net
Advice about free camping in America.

Keycamp

Tel: 0844 406 0200
www.keycamp.co.uk
Family camping holidays in Europe.

Pitch Up

www.pitchup.com
Reviews of campsites in the UK and Ireland with a search facility to help you find the right campsite.

'Glamping'

Featherdown Farms

Tel: 01420 80804
www.featherdown.co.uk
Farms with luxury tents and a focus on outdoor life.

Jardins D'Issil

Tel: 00 212 524 485 711
www.jardinsissil.com
Luxurious tents in Morocco.

Mobile homes and lodges

Center Parcs

Tel: 08448 267723
www.centerparcs.co.uk
Holiday villages with lodge-style accommodation in the UK.

Haven

Tel: 0871 230 1930
www.haven.com
Family-orientated caravan parks in the UK.

Shorefield Parks

www.shorefield.co.uk
Mobile home and lodge holidays in the UK.

Siblu

Tel: 0871 911 2288
www.siblu.com
Mobile home holidays in France, Spain and Italy.

Spas

The following spas all have facilities for children.

Aquacity Poprad, Slovakia

www.aquacity.sk

Azia Resort, Paphos, Cyprus

www.aziaresort.com

Hotel Schwarz, Tyrol, Austria

www.hotel-schwarz.com

La Manga Resort, Murcia, Spain

www.lamangaclub.com

Out of the Blue, Agia Pelagia, Heraklion, Greece

www.capsis.com

Runnymede Hotel, UK

www.runnymedehotel.com

Serenity Spa, Seaham Hall, UK

www.seaham-hall.co.uk

The Vineyard at Stockcross, UK

www.the-vineyard.co.uk

Family-friendly cruise operators

Carnival Cruises

www.carnivalcruise.co.uk

Disney Cruises

disneycruise.disney.go.com

Royal Caribbean International Cruises

www.royalcaribbean.co.uk

Accommodation

BudgetStayUK

www.budgetstayuk.com
Offers accommodation in academic venues.

Holiday Lettings

www.holidaylettings.co.uk
Rent privately-owned self-catering houses and apartments all over the world.

HomeAway Holiday Rentals

www.holiday-rentals.co.uk
A website where people can rent out their holiday homes when it is unoccupied.

Hostel Bookers

www.hostelbookers.com
A great site for researching and booking youth hostels – customers can review where they have stayed which can be useful to look at when making your choice.

Hostel World

www.hostelworld.com
Another hostel booking site. Customers can rate hostels they stay in to help you do your research.

Last Minute

www.lastminute.com
General travel and holidays and bargain 'secret hotels'.

Teletext Holidays

www.teletextholidays.co.uk
Find good holiday bargains and late deals on this website.

Travel.co.uk

www.travel.co.uk
Another site for holiday bargains and late deals.

Travel Supermarket

www.travelsupermarket.com
Independent and impartial comparison of the UK's best travel deals.

University Rooms

www.universityrooms.co.uk
Offers value for money accommodation in academic venues.

Budgeting

Airmiles

www.airmiles.co.uk
Collect points to exchange for flights, hotels and free family days out.

Kayak.co.uk

www.kayak.co.uk
Comparison site for flights, hotels, cars and package holidays.

Mercer's Cost of Living Survey

www.mercer.com/costofliving
Compares the cost of living in cities across the world, useful for your research
when calculating how much spending money to allow.

Money Saving Expert

www.moneysavingexpert.com
Latest tips on saving money, including holidays and travel.

Money Supermarket

www.moneysupermarket.com
Compare prices of all kinds of things, including travel insurance.

Post Office Holiday Costs Barometer

www.royalmail.com
Gives you the cost of items you might buy on holiday in various countries.

Travel Money Max

www.travelmoneymax.com
Helps you find the best place to buy currency.

XE

www.xe.com
Check the latest exchange rates for any currency.

Transport

Carrentals.co.uk

www.carrentals.co.uk
The car hire comparison search engine.

Eurolines

www.eurolines.co.uk
Information on coach travel, routes and costs to Europe.

FerryCheap

Tel: 01304 501100
www.ferrycheap.com
Brings together most of the major ferry operators.

Flying with children

http://flyingwithchildren1.blogspot.com
An excellent blog written by a mother and ex-flight attendant packed with tips about flying with children.

Motorail

www.seat61.com/Motorail.htm
A complete guide to motorail services for UK travellers.

National Express

www.nationalexpress.com
Information on coach travel, routes and costs within the UK.

National Rail Guide

Tel: 08457 48 49 50
www.nationalrail.co.uk
Train times and fares in the UK.

Rail Europe

www.raileurope.co.uk
Train times and fares in Europe, including Eurostar.

Baby and toddler equipment

Bebebel

www.bebebel.co.uk
Deliver your chosen branded baby goods to your holiday accommodation.

Identify Me

www.identifyme.co.uk
Identification bracelets in case your child gets lost.

Complaints

ABTA

www.abta.com
ABTA represents travel agencies and tour operators and aims to maintain high standards of trading practice.

ATOL

www.atol.org.uk
Protection schemes for holidays and flights. May be able to help you if you have a complaint about your holiday or your holiday company goes bust.

Small Claims Court

www.hmcourts-service.gov.uk/infoabout/claims/index.htm
Information about how to make a claim through the small claims court.

Which?

www.which.co.uk
Complaint letter templates and information about how to complain. To find them click on 'Which advice' then 'holiday and leisure' and they are in the section covering compensation.

Miscellaneous and other useful sites

007 Breasts

www.007b.com/public-breastfeeding-world.php
www.007b.com/public-breastfeeding-europe.php
A useful site with information on the attitudes of residents of other countries on breastfeeding in public.

Baby Centre

www.babycentre.co.uk
General baby site – good place to ask advice and opinions from other mums.

Girls' Travel Club

www.girlstravelclub.co.uk
A website with all sorts of beautiful things for girls to take travelling.

Have a Lovely Time

www.havealovelytime.com
Family travel website contributed to by real mums (including the author of this book).

Homeschooling

www.home-schooling-uk.com
Helpful resource if you plan to homeschool your children during an extended trip.

La Leche League

www.laleche.org.uk
May be able to give advice on the attitude to breastfeeding in various parts of the world. The links beneath are also useful.

Moonfruit

www.moonfruit.com
Allows you to build your own website easily and for free.

Netmums

www.netmums.co.uk
Get in touch with other mums to discuss holiday plans. Also has local sections for finding out what's on in your area.

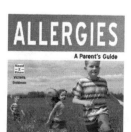

Need - 2 - Know

Available Titles Include ...

Allergies A Parent's Guide
ISBN 978-1-86144-064-8 £8.99

Autism A Parent's Guide
ISBN 978-1-86144-069-3 £8.99

Blood Pressure The Essential Guide
ISBN 978-1-86144-067-9 £8.99

Dyslexia and Other Learning Difficulties
A Parent's Guide ISBN 978-1-86144-042-6 £8.99

Bullying A Parent's Guide
ISBN 978-1-86144-044-0 £8.99

Epilepsy The Essential Guide
ISBN 978-1-86144-063-1 £8.99

Your First Pregnancy The Essential Guide
ISBN 978-1-86144-066-2 £8.99

Gap Years The Essential Guide
ISBN 978-1-86144-079-2 £8.99

Secondary School A Parent's Guide
ISBN 978-1-86144-093-8 £9.99

Primary School A Parent's Guide
ISBN 978-1-86144-088-4 £9.99

Applying to University The Essential Guide
ISBN 978-1-86144-052-5 £8.99

ADHD The Essential Guide
ISBN 978-1-86144-060-0 £8.99

Student Cookbook – Healthy Eating The Essential Guide
ISBN 978-1-86144-069-3 £8.99

Multiple Sclerosis The Essential Guide
ISBN 978-1-86144-086-0 £8.99

Coeliac Disease The Essential Guide
ISBN 978-1-86144-087-7 £9.99

Special Educational Needs A Parent's Guide
ISBN 978-1-86144-116-4 £9.99

The Pill An Essential Guide
ISBN 978-1-86144-058-7 £8.99

University A Survival Guide
ISBN 978-1-86144-072-3 £8.99

View the full range at **www.need2knowbooks.co.uk**.
To order our titles call **01733 898103**, email **sales@ n2kbooks.com** or visit the website. Selected ebooks available online.

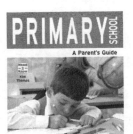
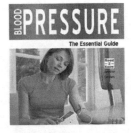
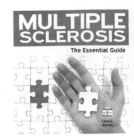

Need - 2 - Know, Remus House, Coltsfoot Drive, Peterborough, PE2 9JX